FREE Study Skills DVD Offer

Dear Customer,

Thank you for your purchase from Mometrix! We consider it an honor and privilege that you have purchased our product and want to ensure your satisfaction.

As a way of showing our appreciation and to help us better serve you, we have developed a Study Skills DVD that we would like to give you for <u>FREE</u>. **This DVD covers our "best practices" for studying for your exam, from using our study materials to preparing for the day of the test.**

All that we ask is that you email us your feedback that would describe your experience so far with our product. Good, bad or indifferent, we want to know what you think!

To get your **FREE Study Skills DVD**, email <u>freedvd@mometrix.com</u> with "FREE STUDY SKILLS DVD" in the subject line and the following information in the body of the email:

   a.   The name of the product you purchased.

   b.   Your product rating on a scale of 1-5, with 5 being the highest rating.

   c.   Your feedback. It can be long, short, or anything in-between, just your impressions and experience so far with our product. Good feedback might include how our study material met your needs and will highlight features of the product that you found helpful.

   d.   Your full name and shipping address where you would like us to send your free DVD.

If you have any questions or concerns, please don't hesitate to contact me directly.

Thanks again!

Sincerely,

Jay Willis
Vice President
<u>jay.willis@mometrix.com</u>
1-800-673-8175

California

POST Exam

SECRETS

Study Guide
Your Key to Exam Success

POST Exam Review for the
California POST Entry-Level Law
Enforcement Test Battery (PELLETB)

Published by
Mometrix Test Preparation
POST Exam Secrets Test Prep Team

Written and edited by the POST Exam Secrets Test Prep Staff

Printed in the United States of America

This paper meets the requirements of ANSI/NISO Z39.48-1992 (Permanence of Paper).

Mometrix offers volume discount pricing to institutions. For more information or a price quote, please contact our sales department at sales@mometrix.com or 888-248-1219.

*Mometrix Media LLC is not affiliated with or endorsed by any official testing organization. All organizational and test names are trademarks of their respective owners.

ISBN 13: 978-1-62733-706-9
ISBN 10: 1-62733-706-7

Dear Future Exam Success Story:

Congratulations on your purchase of our study guide. Our goal in writing our study guide was to cover the content on the test, as well as provide insight into typical test taking mistakes and how to overcome them.

Standardized tests are a key component of being successful, which only increases the importance of doing well in the high-pressure high-stakes environment of test day. How well you do on this test will have a significant impact on your future, and we have the research and practical advice to help you execute on test day.

The product you're reading now is designed to exploit weaknesses in the test itself, and help you avoid the most common errors test takers frequently make.

How to use this study guide

We don't want to waste your time. Our study guide is fast-paced and fluff-free. We suggest going through it a number of times, as repetition is an important part of learning new information and concepts.

First, read through the study guide completely to get a feel for the content and organization. Read the general success strategies first, and then proceed to the content sections. Each tip has been carefully selected for its effectiveness.

Second, read through the study guide again, and take notes in the margins and highlight those sections where you may have a particular weakness.

Finally, bring the manual with you on test day and study it before the exam begins.

Your success is our success

We would be delighted to hear about your success. Send us an email and tell us your story. Thanks for your business and we wish you continued success.

Sincerely,

Mometrix Test Preparation Team

TABLE OF CONTENTS

Top 20 Test Taking Tips

1. Carefully follow all the test registration procedures
2. Know the test directions, duration, topics, question types, how many questions
3. Setup a flexible study schedule at least 3-4 weeks before test day
4. Study during the time of day you are most alert, relaxed, and stress free
5. Maximize your learning style; visual learner use visual study aids, auditory learner use auditory study aids
6. Focus on your weakest knowledge base
7. Find a study partner to review with and help clarify questions
8. Practice, practice, practice
9. Get a good night's sleep; don't try to cram the night before the test
10. Eat a well balanced meal
11. Know the exact physical location of the testing site; drive the route to the site prior to test day
12. Bring a set of ear plugs; the testing center could be noisy
13. Wear comfortable, loose fitting, layered clothing to the testing center; prepare for it to be either cold or hot during the test
14. Bring at least 2 current forms of ID to the testing center
15. Arrive to the test early; be prepared to wait and be patient
16. Eliminate the obviously wrong answer choices, then guess the first remaining choice
17. Pace yourself; don't rush, but keep working and move on if you get stuck
18. Maintain a positive attitude even if the test is going poorly
19. Keep your first answer unless you are positive it is wrong
20. Check your work, don't make a careless mistake

Test Overview

The POST Entry-Level Law Enforcement Test Battery (PELLETB) was developed by the state of California to help ensure that every person who is hired for a law enforcement position in the state is fully qualified to serve in that capacity. (POST stands for Peace Officer Standards and Training.) While a PELLETB score is by no means the only criteria used in determining if a person is a suitable candidate for a law enforcement career in California, it's certainly one of the most important factors in determining if a person has a future in this field.

The position of law enforcement officer is one of the most important jobs in the United States, and it is also one of the noblest careers a person can aspire to. When we hear people talking about public service and wanting to give something back to the community, they are usually politicians talking about their reasons for running for office. Politicians certainly play an important role in society, but a very strong argument can be made that no occupation even comes close to law enforcement officers in terms of giving back to the community and serving the public.

These jobs are also rank very high on the list of the most difficult occupations, and not just physically. Yes, in order to work in law enforcement, a person certainly needs to be physically fit and prepared to deal with a violent attacker at a moment's notice, but the emotional and mental challenges of these jobs can be even more stressful over the course of a person's career. Most people have no idea how much sacrifice and dedication is required of a person who chooses to make this their life work. Law enforcement officers are truly the unsung heroes of our time.

Given how difficult these occupations are, and how little appreciation officers receive from society and the general public these days, it may come as a surprise to learn that competition for these jobs is stiff. If you hope to land one of these positions for yourself, it won't be easy, and you'll have to overcome many hurdles before you can join the ranks of the select few men and women in the front lines of law enforcement. One of the biggest challenges you'll face is making a good score on the POST Entry-Level Law Enforcement Test Battery (PELLETB).

PELLETB is considered an aptitude test; that is, it's not primarily considered a test of knowledge and information one has acquired, but as a measurement of skills and abilities that a person has picked up over a lifetime. Most of the tests you took in high school were the standard kind, where you were asked, for example, to name the city that is the capital of California, or select the year that America declared independence from England. PELLETB isn't that kind of test. Don't get the wrong idea, however – unlike with many aptitude tests, it is definitely possible to raise your potential for a good score on the PELLETB with diligent preparation before you sit down and take the test.

The PELLETB has a time limit of two and a half hours, and it's currently taken only with pencil and paper. There are three components of the exam – Writing Ability, Reading Ability, and Reasoning Ability. In the writing section, there are a total of 45 questions. You'll be given 15 questions measuring your abilities in three different areas, or sub-tests. In the Clarity sub-test, each question will show you two sentences. You'll be asked to decide which sentence does a better job of communicating its intended message correctly. On the Spelling sub-test, each of the 15 questions will show you a word spelled four different ways, and you'll need to select the one that's spelled correctly. In the Vocabulary sub-test of this section, you'll be given a sentence in which one of the words has been underlined. You'll need to select from the answer choices the word that is closest in meaning to the underlined word.

The Reading Ability section contains two sub-tests. The first one features 20 items testing your reading comprehension skills. You'll read a passage, which will be from one to several paragraphs long, and then you'll be asked questions about what you just read to see how well you understood the information in the text. The other sub-test is called a cloze test. This will also feature a passage of written text, and the first sentence and the last sentence will look normal. However, in the sentences in between, every seventh word will missing. Instead, you'll see a series of dashes, with each dash representing a letter of the word that is missing. You'll need to write in the word that is missing. You will need to figure out what word should go there by the context of the sentence and the number of letters in the missing word, represented by the dashes.

The last section of the PELLETB is the Reasoning Ability test, which contains 16 items. These questions will vary. In one common question type, you'll be shown several items, and asked which one doesn't belong. In another, you'll be shown several numbers and asked what the next number in the series will be. This measures your abilities to recognize patterns and relationships, and to understand how things are alike and how they differ.

The PELLETB isn't scored the same way most of the tests you're used to are scored. Your score is called a T-score, and it's based on your test results compared to the results of other test takers. A score of 50 is considered the midpoint, and most people fall somewhere between 40 and 60, which is considered the range of average scores. Very few people score lower than 30 or higher than 70. Most agencies require an applicant to have a score of at least 42 to be considered, but some require scores in the upper 40s or higher. Needless to say, all other factors being equal, the higher your score, the better your chances of being hired. If you take the PELLETB and aren't satisfied with your score, you may retake it after waiting 30 days. However, if you use this guide to help you prepare for your first try, and you give it your best, you should be able to do well on your first attempt at the PELLETB.

Clarity

Clarity simply means *clearness*, and it's another very important aspect of communication, especially written communication. It's vitally important for a peace officer to write in such a way that the meaning of the written communication is crystal clear; there should be no doubt as to the exact meaning. This section will cover the basics of grammar as it relates to clear written communication.

Subjects and Predicates

<u>Subjects</u>
Every sentence has two things: a subject and a verb. The subject of a sentence names who or what the sentence is all about. The subject may be directly stated in a sentence, or the subject may be the implied *you*.

In imperative sentences, the verb's subject is understood (e.g., |You| Run to the store). So, the subject may not be in the sentence. Normally, the subject comes before the verb. However, the subject comes after the verb in sentences that begin with *There are* or *There was*.

Direct:
John knows the way to the park.
(Who knows the way to the park? Answer: John)

The cookies need ten more minutes.
(What needs ten minutes? Answer: The cookies)

By five o' clock, Bill will need to leave.
(Who needs to leave? Answer: Bill)

Remember: The subject can come after the verb.
There are five letters on the table for him.
(What is on the table? Answer: Five letters)

There were coffee and doughnuts in the house.
(What was in the house? Answer: Coffee and doughnuts)

Implied:
Go to the post office for me.
(Who is going to the post office? Answer: You are.)

Come and sit with me, please?
(Who needs to come and sit? Answer: You do.)

The complete subject has the simple subject and all of the modifiers. To find the complete subject, ask *Who* or *What* and insert the verb to complete the question. The answer is the complete subject. To find the simple subject, remove all of the modifiers in the complete subject. When you can find the subject of a sentence, you can correct many problems. These problems include sentence fragments and subject-verb agreement.

Examples:
The small red car is the one that he wants for Christmas.
(The complete subject is *the small red car*.)

The young artist is coming over for dinner.
(The complete subject is *the young artist*.)

> **Review Video: Subjects**
> Visit **mometrix.com/academy** and enter **Code: 444771**

Predicates
In a sentence, you always have a predicate and a subject. A predicate is what remains when you have found the subject. The subject tells what the sentence is about, and the predicate explains or describes the subject.

Think about the sentence: *He sings.* In this sentence, we have a subject (He) and a predicate (sings). This is all that is needed for a sentence to be complete. Would we like more information? Of course, we would like to know more. However, if this all the information that you are given, you have a complete sentence.

Now, let's look at another sentence:
John and Jane sing on Tuesday nights at the dance hall.

What is the subject of this sentence?
Answer: John and Jane.

What is the predicate of this sentence?
Answer: Everything else in the sentence besides John and Jane.

Subject-Verb Agreement

Verbs agree with their subjects in number. In other words, singular subjects need singular verbs. Plural subjects need plural verbs. Singular is for one person, place, or thing. Plural is for more than one person, place, or thing. Subjects and verbs must also agree in person: first, second, or third. The present tense ending -s is used on a verb if its subject is third person singular; otherwise, the verb takes no ending.

> ➤ **Review Video:** <u>Subjects and Verbs</u>
> *Visit* ***mometrix.com/academy*** *and enter* ***Code:*** **479190**

<u>Number Agreement Examples:</u>
Single Subject and Verb: *Dan calls home.*
(Dan is one person. So, the singular verb *calls* is needed.)

Plural Subject and Verb: *Dan and Bob call home.*
(More than one person needs the plural verb *call*.)

<u>Person Agreement Examples:</u>
First Person: I *am* walking.
Second Person: You *are* walking.
Third Person: He *is* walking.

Problems with Subject-Verb Agreement

- <u>Words between Subject and Verb</u>
  The joy of my life returns home tonight.
  (**Singular Subject**: joy. **Singular Verb**: returns)
  The phrase *of my life* does not influence the verb *returns*.

  The question that still remains unanswered is "Who are you?"
  (**Singular Subject**: question. **Singular Verb**: is)
  Don't let the phrase "*that still remains…*" trouble you. The subject question goes with *is*.

- <u>Compound Subjects</u>
  You and Jon are invited to come to my house.
  (**Plural Subject**: You and Jon. **Plural Verb**: are)

  The pencil and paper belong to me.
  (**Plural Subject**: pencil and paper. **Plural Verb**: belong)

- <u>Subjects Joined by *Or* and *Nor*</u>
  Today or tomorrow is the day.
  (**Subject**: Today / tomorrow. **Verb**: is)

Stan or Phil wants to read the book.
(**Subject**: Stan / Phil. **Verb**: wants)

Neither the books nor the *pen is* on the desk.
(**Subject**: Books / Pen. **Verb**: is)

Either the blanket or *pillows arrive* this afternoon.
(**Subject**: Blanket / Pillows. **Verb**: arrive)

Note: Singular subjects that are joined with the conjunction *or* need a singular verb. However, when one subject is singular and another is plural, you make the verb agree with the closer subject. The example about books and the pen has a singular verb because the pen (singular subject) is closer to the verb.

- Indefinite Pronouns: Either, Neither, and Each
  Is either of you ready for the game?
  (**Singular Subject**: Either. **Singular Verb**: is)

  Each man, woman, and child is unique.
  (**Singular Subject**: Each. **Singular Verb**: is)

- The adjective Every and compounds: Everybody, Everyone, Anybody, Anyone
  Every day passes faster than the last.
  (**Singular Subject**: Every day. **Singular Verb**: passes)

  Anybody is welcome to bring a tent.
  (**Singular Subject**: Anybody. **Singular Verb**: is)

- Collective Nouns
  The family eats at the restaurant every Friday night.
  (The members of the family are one at the restaurant.)

  The team are leaving for their homes after the game.
  (The members of the team are leaving as individuals to go to their own homes.)

- Who, Which, and That as Subject
  This is the man who is helping me today.
  He is a good man who serves others before himself.
  This painting that is hung over the couch is very beautiful.

- Plural Form and Singular Meaning
  Some nouns that are singular in meaning but plural in form: news, mathematics, physics, and economics
    The news is coming on now.
    Mathematics is my favorite class.

Some nouns that are plural in meaning: athletics, gymnastics, scissors, and pants
Do these pants come with a shirt?
The scissors are for my project.

Note: Look to your dictionary for help when you aren't sure whether a noun with a plural form has a singular or plural meaning.

Addition, Multiplication, Subtraction, and Division are normally singular.
One plus one is two.
Three times three is nine.

Complements

A complement is a noun, pronoun, or adjective that is used to give more information about the verb in the sentence.

Direct Objects
A direct object is a noun that takes or receives the action of a verb. Remember: a complete sentence does not need a direct object. A sentence needs only a subject and a verb. When you are looking for a direct object, find the verb and ask *who* or *what*.
Example: I took the blanket. (Who or what did I take? *The blanket*)
Jane read books. (Who or what does Jane read? *Books*)

Indirect Objects
An indirect object is a word or group of words that show how an action had an influence on someone or something. If there is an indirect object in a sentence, then you always have a direct object in the sentence. When you are looking for the indirect object, find the verb and ask *to/for whom or what*.
Examples: We taught the old dog a new trick.
(To/For Whom or What was taught? *The old dog*)

I gave them a math lesson.
(To/For Whom or What was given? *Them*)

Predicate Nouns are nouns that modify the subject and finish linking verbs.
Example: My father is a lawyer.
Father is the subject. Lawyer is the predicate noun.

Predicate Adjectives are adjectives that modify the subject and finish linking verbs.
Example: Your mother is patient.
Mother is the subject. Patient is the predicate adjective.

Pronoun Usage

Pronoun - antecedent agreement - The antecedent is the noun that has been replaced by a pronoun. A pronoun and the antecedent agree when they are singular or plural.

Singular agreement: *John* came into town, and *he* played for us.
(The word *He* replaces *John*.)

Plural agreement: *John and Rick* came into town, and *they* played for us.
(The word *They* replaces *John* and *Rick*.)

To know the correct pronoun for a compound subject, try each pronoun separately with the verb. Your knowledge of pronouns will tell you which one is correct.
Example: Bob and (I, me) will be going.
(Answer: Bob and I will be going.)

Test: (1) *I will be going* or (2) *Me will be going*. The second choice cannot be correct because *me* is not used as a subject of a sentence. Instead, *me* is used as an object.

When a pronoun is used with a noun immediately following (as in "we boys"), try the sentence without the added noun.
Example: (We/Us) boys played football last year.
(Answer: We boys played football last year.)

Test: (1) *We* played football last year or (2) *Us* played football last year. Again, the second choice cannot be correct because *us* is not used as a subject of a sentence. Instead, *us* is used as an object.

> ➤ **Review Video: Pronoun Usage**
> *Visit **mometrix.com/academy** and enter **Code: 666500***

Pronoun reference - A pronoun should point clearly to the antecedent. Here is how a pronoun reference can be unhelpful if it is not directly stated or puzzling.

Unhelpful: Ron and Jim went to the store, and he bought soda.
(Who bought soda? Ron or Jim?)

Helpful: Jim went to the store, and he bought soda.
(The sentence is clear. Jim bought the soda.)

Personal pronouns - Some pronouns change their form by their placement in a sentence. A pronoun that is a subject in a sentence comes in the subjective case. Pronouns that serve as objects appear in the objective case. Finally, the pronouns that are used as possessives appear in the possessive case.

Subjective case: *He* is coming to the show.
(The pronoun *He* is the subject of the sentence.)

Objective case: Josh drove *him* to the airport.
(The pronoun *him* is the object of the sentence.)

Possessive case: The flowers are *mine*.
(The pronoun *mine* shows ownership of the flowers.)

Who or whom – *Who*, a subjective-case pronoun, can be used as a subject. *Whom*, an objective case pronoun, can be used as an object. The words *who* and *whom* are common in subordinate clauses or in questions.

Subject: He knows who wants to come.
(*Who* is the subject of the verb *wants*.)

Object: He knows whom we want at the party.
(*Whom* is the object of *we want*.)

Sentence Structures

The four major types of sentence structure are:
1. Simple Sentences - Simple sentences have one independent clause with no subordinate clauses. A simple sentence can have compound elements (e.g., a compound subject or verb).
   Examples:
   Judy watered the lawn. (Singular Subject & Singular Predicate)
   Judy and Alan watered the lawn. (Compound Subject: Judy and Alan)

2. Compound Sentences - Compound sentences have two or more independent clauses with no dependent clauses. Usually, the independent clauses are joined with a comma and a coordinating conjunction, or they can be joined with a semicolon.
   Example:
   The time has come, and we are ready.
   I woke up at dawn; then I went outside to watch the sun rise.

3. Complex Sentences - A complex sentence has one independent clause and one or more dependent clauses.
   Examples:
   Although he had the flu, Harry went to work.
   Marcia got married after she finished college.

4. Compound-Complex Sentences - A compound-complex sentence has at least two independent clauses and at least one dependent clause.
Examples:
John is my friend who went to India, and he brought souvenirs for us.
You may not know, but we heard the music that you played last night.

> **Review Video:** <u>Sentence Structure</u>
*Visit **mometrix.com/academy** and enter **Code: 700478***

Sentence Fragments

A part of a sentence should not be treated like a complete sentence. A sentence must be made of at least one independent clause. An independent clause has a subject and a verb. Remember that the independent clause can stand alone as a sentence. Some fragments are independent clauses that begin with a subordinating word (e.g., as, because, so, etc.). Other fragments may not have a subject, a verb, or both.

A sentence fragment can be repaired in several ways. One way is to put the fragment with a neighbor sentence. Another way is to be sure that punctuation is not needed. You can also turn the fragment into a sentence by adding any missing pieces. Sentence fragments are allowed for writers who want to show off their art. However, for your exam, sentence fragments are not allowed.

Fragment: Because he wanted to sail for Rome.
Correct: He dreamed of Europe because he wanted to sail for Rome.

Dangling and Misplaced Modifiers

Dangling Modifiers
A dangling modifier is a verbal phrase that does not have a clear connection to a word. A dangling modifier can also be a dependent clause (the subject and/or verb are not included) that does not have a clear connection to a word.

Examples:
Dangling: *Reading each magazine article*, the stories caught my attention.
Corrected: Reading each magazine article, *I* was entertained by the stories.

In this example, the word *stories* cannot be modified by *Reading each magazine article*. People can read, but stories cannot read. So, the pronoun *I* is needed for the modifying phrase *Reading each magazine article*.

Dangling: Since childhood, my grandparents have visited me for Christmas.
Corrected: Since childhood, I have been visited by my grandparents for Christmas.

In this example, the dependent adverb clause *Since childhood* cannot modify grandparents. So, the pronoun *I* is needed for the modifying adverb clause.

<u>Misplaced Modifiers</u>
In some sentences, a modifier can be put in more than one place. However, you need to be sure that there is no confusion about which word is being explained or given more detail.

Incorrect: He read the book to a crowd that was filled with beautiful pictures.
Correct: He read the book that was filled with beautiful pictures to a crowd.

The crowd is not filled with pictures. The book is filled with pictures.

Incorrect: John only ate fruits and vegetables for two weeks.
Correct: John ate *only* fruits and vegetables for two weeks.

John may have done nothing else for two weeks but eat fruits and vegetables and sleep. However, it is reasonable to think that John had fruits and vegetables for his meals. Then, he continued to work on other things.

Run-on Sentences

Run-on sentences are independent clauses that have not been joined by a conjunction. When two or more independent clauses appear in one sentence, they must be joined in one of these ways:
1. Correction with a comma and a coordinating conjunction.
   Incorrect: I went on the trip and I had a good time.
   Correct: I went on the trip, and I had a good time.

2. Correction with a semicolon, a colon, or a dash. Used when independent clauses are closely related and their connection is clear without a coordinating conjunction.
   Incorrect: I went to the store and I bought some eggs.
   Correct: I went to the store; I bought some eggs.

3. Correction by separating sentences. This correction may be used when both independent clauses are long. Also, this can be used when one sentence is a question and one is not.
   Incorrect: The drive to New York takes ten hours it makes me very tired.
   Correct: The drive to New York takes ten hours. So, I become very tired.

4. Correction by changing parts of the sentence. One way is to turn one of the independent clauses into a phrase or subordinate clause.
   Incorrect: The drive to New York takes ten hours it makes me very tired.
   Correct: During the ten hour drive to New York, I become very tired.

Note: Normally, one of these choices will be a clear correction to a run-on sentence. The fourth way can be the best correction but needs the most work.

Spelling

Peace officers must have very good spelling skills. Writing reports is an important part of the job, and there are other aspects of the job that also require written communication. Without the ability to spell properly an officer would not be able to write a good report. At best, bad spelling looks unprofessional; at worst, it can lead to misunderstandings, which could cause even bigger problems.

Rules of Spelling

Words ending with a consonant
Usually the final consonant is doubled on a word before adding a suffix. This is the rule for single syllable words, words ending with one consonant, and multi-syllable words with the last syllable accented. The following are examples:
- *beg* becomes *begging* (single syllable)
- *shop* becomes *shopped* (single syllable)
- *add* becomes *adding* (already ends in double consonant, do not add another *d*)
- *deter* becomes *deterring* (multi-syllable, accent on last syllable)
- *regret* becomes *regrettable* (multi-syllable, accent on last syllable)
- *compost* becomes *composting* (do not add another *t* because the accent is on the first syllable)

Words ending with *y* or *c*
The general rule for words ending in *y* is to keep the *y* when adding a suffix if the *y* is preceded by a vowel. If the word ends in a consonant and *y* the *y* is changed to an *i* before the suffix is added (unless the suffix itself begins with *i*). The following are examples:
- *pay* becomes *paying* (keep the *y*)
- *bully* becomes *bullied* (change to *i*)
- *bully* becomes *bullying* (keep the *y* because the suffix is –*ing*)

If a word ends with *c* and the suffix begins with an *e, i,* or *y*, the letter *k* is usually added to the end of the word. The following are examples:
- *panic* becomes *panicky*
- *mimic* becomes *mimicking*

Words containing *ie* or *ei,* and/or ending with *e*
Most words are spelled with an *i* before *e*, except when they follow the letter *c,* **or** sound like *a*. For example, the following words are spelled correctly according to these rules:
- piece, friend, believe (*i* before *e*)
- receive, ceiling, conceited (except after *c*)
- weight, neighborhood, veil (sounds like *a*)

To add a suffix to words ending with the letter *e*, first determine if the *e* is silent. If it is, the *e* will be kept if the added suffix begins with a consonant. If the suffix begins with a vowel, the *e* is dropped. The following are examples:

- *age* becomes *ageless* (keep the *e*)
- *age* becomes *aging* (drop the *e*)

An exception to this rule occurs when the word ends in *ce* or *ge* and the suffix *able* or *ous* is added; these words will retain the letter *e*. The following are examples:

- *courage* becomes *courageous*
- *notice* becomes *noticeable*

<u>Words ending with *ise* or *ize*</u>
A small number of words end with *ise*. Most of the words in the English language with the same sound end in *ize*. The following are examples:

- advertise, advise, arise, chastise, circumcise, and comprise
- compromise, demise, despise, devise, disguise, enterprise, excise, and exercise
- franchise, improvise, incise, merchandise, premise, reprise, and revise
- supervise, surmise, surprise, and televise

Words that end with *ize* include the following:

- accessorize, agonize, authorize, and brutalize
- capitalize, caramelize, categorize, civilize, and demonize
- downsize, empathize, euthanize, idolize, and immunize
- legalize, metabolize, mobilize, organize, and ostracize
- plagiarize, privatize, utilize, and visualize

(Note that some words may technically be spelled with *ise*, especially in British English, but it is more common to use *ize*. Examples include *symbolize/symbolise*, and *baptize/baptise*.)

<u>Words ending with *ceed, sede,* or *cede*</u>
There are only three words that end with *ceed* in the English language: *exceed, proceed,* and *succeed*. There is only one word that ends with *sede*, and that word is *supersede*. Many other words that sound like *sede* actually end with *cede*. The following are examples:

- concede, recede, and precede

<u>Words ending in *able* or *ible*</u>
For words ending in *able* or *ible*, there are no hard and fast rules. The following are examples:

- adjustable, unbeatable, collectable, deliverable, and likeable
- edible, compatible, feasible, sensible, and credible

There are more words ending in *able* than *ible*; this is useful to know if guessing is necessary.

Words ending in *ance* or *ence*
The suffixes *ence, ency,* and *ent* are used in the following cases:
- the suffix is preceded by the letter *c* but sounds like *s* – *innocence*
- the suffix is preceded by the letter *g* but sounds like *j* – *intelligence, negligence*

The suffixes *ance, ancy,* and *ant* are used in the following cases:
- the suffix is preceded by the letter *c* but sounds like *k* – *significant, vacant*
- the suffix is preceded by the letter *g* with a hard sound - *elegant, extravagance*

If the suffix is preceded by other letters, there are no steadfast rules. For example: *finance, elegance,* and *defendant* use the letter *a*, while *respondent, competence,* and *excellent* use the letter *e*.

Words ending in *tion, sion,* or *cian*
Words ending in *tion, sion,* or *cian* all sound like *shun* or *zhun*. There are no rules for which ending is used for words. The following are examples:
- action, agitation, caution, fiction, nation, and motion
- admission, expression, mansion, permission, and television
- electrician, magician, musician, optician, and physician (note that these words tend to describe occupations)

Words with the *ai* or *ia* combination
When deciding if *ai* or *ia* is correct, the combination of *ai* usually sounds like one vowel sound, as in *Britain*, while the vowels in *ia* are pronounced separately, as in *guardian*. The following are examples:
- captain, certain, faint, hair, malaise, and praise (*ai* makes one sound)
- bacteria, beneficiary, diamond, humiliation, and nuptial (*ia* makes two sounds)

Plural Forms of Nouns

Nouns ending in *ch, sh, s, x,* or *z*
When a noun ends in the letters *ch, sh, s, x,* or *z*, an *es* instead of a singular *s* is added to the end of the word to make it plural. The following are examples:
- *church* becomes *churches*
- *bush* becomes *bushes*
- *bass* becomes *basses*
- *mix* becomes *mixes*
- *buzz* becomes *buzzes*

This is the rule with proper names as well; the Ross family would become the Rosses.

Nouns ending in *y* or *ay/ey/iy/oy/uy*
If a noun ends with a consonant and *y*, the plural is formed by replacing the *y* with *ies*. For example, *fly* becomes *flies* and *puppy* becomes *puppies*. If a noun ends with a vowel and *y*,

the plural is formed by adding an *s*. For example, *alley* becomes *alleys* and *boy* becomes *boys*.

Nouns ending in *f* or *fe*
Most nouns ending in *f* or *fe* are pluralized by replacing the *f* with *v* and adding *es*. The following are examples:
- *knife* becomes *knives; self* becomes *selves; wolf* becomes *wolves.*

An exception to this rule is the word *roof; roof* becomes *roofs.*

Nouns ending in *o*
Most nouns ending with a consonant and *o* are pluralized by adding *es*. The following are examples:
- *hero* becomes *heroes; tornado* becomes *tornadoes; potato* becomes *potatoes*

Most nouns ending with a vowel and *o* are pluralized by adding *s*. The following are examples:
- *portfolio* becomes *portfolios; radio* becomes *radios; shoe* becomes *shoes.*

An exception to these rules is seen with musical terms ending in *o*. These words are pluralized by adding *s* even if they end in a consonant and *o*. The following are examples: *soprano* becomes *sopranos; banjo* becomes *banjos; piano* becomes *pianos.*

Exceptions to the Rules of Plurals

Some words do not fall into any specific category for making the singular form plural. They are irregular. Certain words become plural by changing the vowels within the word. The following are examples:
- *woman* becomes *women; goose* becomes *geese; foot* becomes *feet*

Some words become completely different words in the plural form. The following are examples:
- *mouse* becomes *mice; fungus* becomes *fungi; alumnus* becomes *alumni*

Some words are the same in both the singular and plural forms. The following are examples:
- *Salmon, species,* and *deer* are all the same whether singular or plural.

Vocabulary

Your vocabulary is simply all the words you understand and use. Knowing the meanings of a large number of words, and how to use them, is important for success in a career as a peace officer. You'll be communicating both in speech and in writing with your fellow officers, your superiors, and the general public. Not being able to understand what someone else means would be a serious roadblock to successfully carrying out your duties, as would not being able to communicate precisely and efficiently.

An understanding of the basics of language is helpful--and often vital--to understanding what you read. The term **structural analysis** refers to looking at the parts of a word and breaking down the word into its different components to determine the word's meaning. Parts of a word include prefixes, suffixes, and root words. By learning the meanings of prefixes, suffixes, and other word fundamentals, you can decipher the meaning of words which may not yet be in your vocabulary.

Prefixes are common letter combinations at the beginning of words, while suffixes are common letter combinations at the end of words. The main part of the word is known as the root. Visually, a word would look like this: prefix + root word + suffix. Look first at the individual meanings of the root word, prefix and/or suffix. Use your knowledge of the meaning(s) of the prefix and/or suffix to see what information they add to the root. If the meaning of the root is unknown, one can use knowledge of a prefix and/or suffix meaning to determine an approximate meaning of a word. For example, if you see the word *uninspired* and do not know the meaning, then you can use the knowledge that *un-* means 'not' and discern that the full word means *not inspired*. Learning the common prefixes and suffixes can illuminate at least part of the meaning of an unfamiliar word.

> ➤ **Review Video:** <u>Determining Word Meanings</u>
> *Visit **mometrix.com/academy** and enter **Code: 894894***

Below is a list of common prefixes and their meanings:

Prefixes for Amount

Prefix	Definition	Examples
bi-	two	bisect, biennial
mono-	one, single	monogamy, monologue
poly-	many	polymorphous, polygamous
semi-	half, partly	semicircle, semicolon
uni-	one	uniform, unity

Prefixes for Time and Space

Prefix	Definition	Examples
a-	in, on, of, up, to	abed, afoot
ab-	from, away, off	abdicate, abjure
ad-	to, toward	advance, adventure
ante-	before, previous	antecedent, antedate
anti-	against, opposing	antipathy, antidote
cata-	down, away, thoroughly	catastrophe, cataclysm
circum-	around	circumspect, circumference
com-	with, together, very	commotion, complicate
contra-	against, opposing	contradict, contravene
de-	from	depart
dia-	through, across, apart	diameter, diagnose
dis-	away, off, down, not	dissent, disappear
epi-	upon	epilogue
ex-	out	extract, excerpt
hypo-	under, beneath	hypodermic, hypothesis
inter-	among, between	intercede, interrupt
intra-	within	intramural, intrastate
ob-	against, opposing	objection
per-	through	perceive, permit
peri-	around	periscope, perimeter
post-	after, following	postpone, postscript
pre-	before, previous	prevent, preclude
pro-	forward, in place of	propel, pronoun
retro-	back, backward	retrospect, retrograde
sub-	under, beneath	subjugate, substitute
super-	above, extra	supersede, supernumerary
trans-	across, beyond, over	transact, transport
ultra-	beyond, excessively	ultramodern, ultrasonic, ultraviolet

Prefixes of Negation

Prefix	Definition	Examples
a-	without, lacking	atheist, agnostic
in-	not, opposing	incapable, ineligible
non-	not	nonentity, nonsense
un-	not, reverse of	unhappy, unlock

Miscellaneous Prefixes

Prefix	Definition	Examples
belli-	war, warlike	bellicose
bene-	well, good	benefit, benefactor
equi-	equal	equivalent, equilibrium

for-	away, off, from	forget, forswear
fore-	previous	foretell, forefathers
homo-	same, equal	homogenized, homonym
hyper-	excessive, over	hypercritical, hypertension
in-	in, into	intrude, invade
magn-	large	magnitude, magnify
mal-	bad, poorly, not	malfunction, malpractice
mis-	bad, poorly, not	misspell, misfire
mor-	death	mortality, mortuary
neo-	new	Neolithic, neoconservative
omni-	all, everywhere	omniscient, omnivore
ortho-	right, straight	orthogonal, orthodox
over-	above	overbearing, oversight
pan-	all, entire	panorama, pandemonium
para-	beside, beyond	parallel, paradox
phil-	love, like	philosophy, philanthropic
prim-	first, early	primitive, primary
re-	backward, again	revoke, recur
sym-	with, together	sympathy, symphony
vis-	to see	visage, visible

Below is a list of common suffixes and their meanings:

Adjective Suffixes

Suffix	Definition	Examples
-able (-ible)	capable of being	toler*able*, ed*ible*
-esque	in the style of, like	picturesque, grotesque
-ful	filled with, marked by	thankful, zestful
-ic	make, cause	terrific, beatific
-ish	suggesting, like	churlish, childish
-less	lacking, without	hopeless, countless
-ous	marked by, given to	religious, riotous

Noun Suffixes

Suffix	Definition	Examples
-acy	state, condition	accuracy, privacy
-ance	act, condition, fact	acceptance, vigilance
-ard	one that does excessively	drunkard, sluggard
-ation	action, state, result	occupation, starvation
-dom	state, rank, condition	serfdom, wisdom
-er (-or)	office, action	teach*er*, elevat*or*, hon*or*
-ess	feminine	waitress, duchess
-hood	state, condition	manhood, statehood
-ion	action, result, state	union, fusion

-ism	act, manner, doctrine	barbarism, socialism
-ist	worker, follower	monopolist, socialist
-ity (-ty)	state, quality, condition	acid*ity*, civil*ity*, twen*ty*
-ment	result, action	refreshment, disappointment
-ness	quality, state	greatness, tallness
-ship	position	internship, statesmanship
-sion (-tion)	state, result	revi*sion*, expedi*tion*
-th	act, state, quality	warmth, width
-tude	quality, state, result	magnitude, fortitude

Verb Suffixes

Suffix	Definition	Examples
-ate	having, showing	separate, desolate
-en	cause to be, become	deepen, strengthen
-fy	make, cause to have	glorify, fortify
-ize	cause to be, treat with	sterilize, mechanize, criticize

> ➤ **Review Video: Prefixes, Suffixes, and Root Words**
> *Visit **mometrix.com/academy** and enter **Code: 896380***

Readers of all levels will encounter words that they have either never seen or encountered on a limited basis. The best way to define a word in **context** is to look for nearby words that can assist in learning the meaning of the word. For instance, unfamiliar nouns are often accompanied by examples that provide a definition. Consider the following sentence: *Dave arrived at the party in hilarious garb: a leopard-print shirt, buckskin trousers, and high heels.* If a reader was unfamiliar with the meaning of garb, he or she could read the examples (i.e., a leopard-print shirt, buckskin trousers, and high heels) and quickly determine that the word means *clothing*. Examples will not always be this obvious. Consider this sentence: *Parsley, lemon, and flowers were just a few of items he used as garnishes.* Here, the word *garnishes* is exemplified by parsley, lemon, and flowers. Readers who have eaten in a few restaurants will probably be able to identify a garnish as something used to decorate a plate.

> ➤ **Review Video: Context**
> *Visit **mometrix.com/academy** and enter **Code: 613660***

In addition to looking at the context of a passage, readers can use contrasts to define an unfamiliar word in context. In many sentences, the author will not describe the unfamiliar word directly; instead, he or she will describe the opposite of the unfamiliar word. Thus, you are provided with some information that will bring you closer to defining the word. Consider the following example: *Despite his intelligence, Hector's low brow and bad posture made him look obtuse.* The author writes that Hector's appearance does not convey intelligence. Therefore, *obtuse* must mean unintelligent. Here is another example: *Despite the horrible weather, we were beatific about our trip to Alaska.* The word *despite* indicates that the speaker's feelings were at odds with the weather. Since the weather is described as *horrible*, then *beatific* must mean something positive.

In some cases, there will be very few contextual clues to help a reader define the meaning of an unfamiliar word. When this happens, one strategy that readers may employ is **substitution**. A good reader will brainstorm some possible synonyms for the given word, and he or she will substitute these words into the sentence. If the sentence and the surrounding passage continue to make sense, then the substitution has revealed at least some information about the unfamiliar word. Consider the sentence: *Frank's admonition rang in her ears as she climbed the mountain.* A reader unfamiliar with *admonition* might come up with some substitutions like *vow, promise, advice, complaint*, or *compliment*. All of these words make general sense of the sentence though their meanings are diverse. The process has suggested; however, that an admonition is some sort of message. The substitution strategy is rarely able to pinpoint a precise definition, but this process can be effective as a last resort.

Occasionally, you will be able to define an unfamiliar word by looking at the descriptive words in the context. Consider the following sentence: *Fred dragged the recalcitrant boy kicking and screaming up the stairs.* The words *dragged, kicking,* and *screaming* all suggest that the boy does not want to go up the stairs. The reader may assume that *recalcitrant* means something like unwilling or protesting. In this example, an unfamiliar adjective was identified.

Additionally, using description to define an unfamiliar noun is a common practice compared to unfamiliar adjectives, as in this sentence: *Don's wrinkled frown and constantly shaking fist identified him as a curmudgeon of the first order.* Don is described as having a *wrinkled frown and constantly shaking fist* suggesting that a *curmudgeon* must be a grumpy man. Contrasts do not always provide detailed information about the unfamiliar word, but they at least give the reader some clues.

When a word has more than one meaning, readers can have difficulty with determining how the word is being used in a given sentence. For instance, the verb *cleave*, can mean either *join* or *separate*. When readers come upon this word, they will have to select the definition that makes the most sense. Consider the following sentence: *Hermione's knife cleaved the bread cleanly.* Since, a knife cannot join bread together, the word must indicate separation. A slightly more difficult example would be the sentence: *The birds cleaved together as they flew from the oak tree.* Immediately, the presence of the word *together* should suggest that in this sentence *cleave* is being used to mean *join*. Discovering the intent of a word with multiple meanings requires the same tricks as defining an unknown word: look for contextual clues and evaluate the substituted words.

When you understand how words relate to each other, you will discover more in a passage. This is explained by understanding **synonyms** (e.g., words that mean the same thing) and **antonyms** (e.g., words that mean the opposite of one another). As an example, *dry* and *arid* are synonyms, and *dry* and *wet* are antonyms. There are many pairs of words in English that can be considered synonyms, despite having slightly different definitions. For instance, the words *friendly* and *collegial* can both be used to describe a warm interpersonal relationship, and one would be correct to call them synonyms. However, *collegial* (kin to *colleague*) is often used in reference to professional or academic relationships, and *friendly* has no such connotation. If the difference between the two words is too great, then they should not be called synonyms. *Hot* and *warm* are not synonyms because their meanings are too distinct. A good way to determine whether two words are synonyms is to substitute one word for the other word and verify that the meaning of the sentence has not changed. Substituting *warm* for *hot* in a sentence would convey a different meaning. Although warm and hot may seem close in meaning, warm generally means that the temperature is moderate, and hot generally means that the temperature is excessively high.

Antonyms are words with opposite meanings. *Light* and *dark*, *up* and *down*, *right* and *left*, *good* and *bad*: these are all sets of antonyms. Be careful to distinguish between antonyms and pairs of words that are simply different. *Black* and *gray*, for instance, are not antonyms because gray is not the opposite of black. *Black* and *white*, on the other hand, are antonyms. Not every word has an antonym. For instance, many nouns do not: What would be the antonym of chair? During your exam, the questions related to antonyms are more likely to concern adjectives. You will recall that adjectives are words that describe a noun. Some common adjectives include *purple*, *fast*, *skinny*, and *sweet*. From those four adjectives, *purple* is the item that lacks a group of obvious antonyms.

> **Review Video:** Synonyms and Antonyms
*Visit **mometrix.com/academy** and enter **Code:** 105612*

Reading Ability

Reading Comprehension

For all peace officers, reading is an important part of the job and reading comprehension skills are critical to your success in this occupation. Whether you're reading memos, reports, rules and regulations, or any of the many other kinds of reading material you'll encounter on your job, it's imperative that you have the ability to understand and process the material. While these abilities are necessary for everyone working in law enforcement, anyone who wants to be promoted to higher positions in this field must have extremely strong reading comprehension skills.

Types of Passages

An **expository** passage aims to inform and enlighten readers. The passage is nonfiction and usually centers around a simple, easily defined topic. Since the goal of exposition is to teach, such a passage should be as clear as possible. Often, an expository passage contains helpful organizing words, like *first*, *next*, *for example*, and *therefore*. These words keep the reader oriented in the text. Although expository passages do not need to feature colorful language and artful writing, they are often more effective with these features. For a reader, the challenge of expository passages is to maintain steady attention. Expository passages are not always about subjects that will naturally interest a reader, and the writer is often more concerned with clarity and comprehensibility than with engaging the reader. By reading actively, you will ensure a good habit of focus when reading an expository passage.

> ➤ **Review Video: Expository Passages**
> Visit *mometrix.com/academy* and enter *Code:* **256515**

A **technical** passage is written to describe a complex object or process. Technical writing is common in medical and technological fields, in which complex ideas of mathematics, science, and engineering need to be explained simply and clearly. To ease comprehension, a technical passage usually proceeds in a very logical order. Technical passages often have clear headings and subheadings, which are used to keep the reader oriented in the text. Additionally, you will find that these passages divide sections up with numbers or letters. Many technical passages look more like an outline than a piece of prose. The amount of jargon or difficult vocabulary will vary in a technical passage depending on the intended audience. As much as possible, technical passages try to avoid language that the reader will have to research in order to understand the message, yet readers will find that jargon cannot always be avoided.

> ➤ **Review Video: A Technical Passage**
> Visit *mometrix.com/academy* and enter *Code:* **478923**

Organization of the Text

The way a text is organized can help readers to understand the author's intent and his or her conclusions. There are various ways to organize a text, and each one has a purpose and use.

Some nonfiction texts are organized to **present a problem** followed by a solution. For this type of text, the problem is often explained before the solution is offered. In some cases, as when the problem is well known, the solution may be introduced briefly at the beginning. Other passages may focus on the solution, and the problem will be referenced only occasionally. Some texts will outline multiple solutions to a problem, leaving readers to choose among them. If the author has an interest or an allegiance to one solution, he or she may fail to mention or describe accurately some of the other solutions. Readers should be careful of the author's agenda when reading a problem-solution text. Only by understanding the author's perspective and interests can one develop a proper judgment of the proposed solution.

Occasionally, authors will organize information logically in a passage so the reader can follow and locate the information within the text. Since this is not always the case with passages in an exam, you need to be familiar with other examples of provided information. Two common organizational structures are cause and effect and chronological order. When using **chronological order**, the author presents information in the order that it happened. For example, biographies are written in chronological order. The subject's birth and childhood are presented first, followed by their adult life, and lastly by the events leading up to the person's death.

In **cause and effect**, an author presents one thing that makes something else happen. For example, if one were to go to bed very late and awake very early, then they would be tired in the morning. The cause is lack of sleep, with the effect of being tired the next day.

Identifying the cause-and-effect relationships in a text can be tricky, but there are a few ways to approach this task. Often, these relationships are signaled with certain terms. When an author uses words like *because, since, in order*, and *so*, he or she is likely describing a cause-and-effect relationship. Consider the sentence: *He called her because he needed the homework*. This is a simple causal relationship in which the cause was his need for the homework, and the effect was his phone call. Yet, not all cause-and-effect relationships are marked in this way. Consider the sentences: *He called her. He needed the homework*. When the cause-and-effect relationship is not indicated with a keyword, the relationship can be discovered by asking why something happened. He called her: why? The answer is in the next sentence: He needed the homework.

Many texts follow the **compare-and-contrast** model in which the similarities and differences between two ideas or things are explored. Analysis of the similarities between ideas is called comparison. In an ideal comparison, the author places ideas or things in an equivalent structure (i.e., the author presents the ideas in the same way). If an author wants to show the similarities between cricket and baseball, then he or she may do so by summarizing the equipment and rules for each game. Be mindful of the similarities as they appear in the passage and take note of any differences that are mentioned. Often, these small differences will only reinforce the more general similarity.

Thinking critically about ideas and conclusions can seem like a daunting task. One way to ease this task is to understand the basic elements of ideas and writing techniques. Looking at the way different ideas relate to each other can be a good way for readers to begin their analysis. For instance, sometimes authors will write about two ideas that are in opposition to each other. Or one author will provide his or her ideas on a topic, and another author may respond in opposition. The analysis of these opposing ideas is known as **contrast**. Contrast is often marred by the author's obvious partiality to one of the ideas. A discerning reader will be put off by an author who does not engage in a fair fight. In an analysis of opposing ideas, both ideas should be presented in clear and reasonable terms. If the author does prefer a side, you need to read carefully to determine the areas where the author shows or avoids this preference. In an analysis of opposing ideas, you should proceed through the passage by marking the major differences point by point with an eye that is looking for an explanation of each side's view. For instance, in an analysis of capitalism and communism, there is an importance in outlining each side's view on labor, markets, prices, personal responsibility, etc. Additionally, as you read through the passages, you should note whether the opposing views present each side in a similar manner.

Purposes for Writing

In order to be an effective reader, one must pay attention to the author's **position** and purpose. Even those texts that seem objective and impartial, like textbooks, have a position and bias. Readers need to take these positions into account when considering the author's message. When an author uses emotional language or clearly favors one side of an argument, his or her position is clear. However, the author's position may be evident not only in what he or she writes, but also in what he or she doesn't write. In a normal setting, a reader would want to review some other texts on the same topic in order to develop a view of the author's position. If this was not possible, then you would want to acquire some background about the author. However, since you are in the middle of an exam and the only source of information is the text, you should look for language and argumentation that seems to indicate a particular stance on the subject.

> ➤ **Review Video:** <u>Author's Position</u>
> *Visit **mometrix.com/academy** and enter **Code: 478923***

Usually, identifying the **purpose** of an author is easier than identifying his or her position. In most cases, the author has no interest in hiding his or her purpose. A text that is meant to entertain, for instance, should be written to please the reader. Most narratives, or stories, are written to entertain, though they may also inform or persuade. Informative texts are easy to identify, while the most difficult purpose of a text to identify is persuasion because the author has an interest in making this purpose hard to detect. When a reader discovers that the author is trying to persuade, he or she should be skeptical of the argument. For this reason persuasive texts often try to establish an entertaining tone and hope to amuse the reader into agreement. On the other hand, an informative tone may be implemented to create an appearance of authority and objectivity.

An author's purpose is evident often in the organization of the text (e.g., section headings in bold font points to an informative text). However, you may not have such organization available to you in your exam. Instead, if the author makes his or her main idea clear from the beginning, then the likely purpose of the text is to inform. If the author begins by making a claim and provides various arguments to support that claim, then the purpose is probably to persuade. If the author tells a story or seems to want the attention of the reader more than to push a particular point or deliver information, then his or her purpose is most likely to entertain. As a reader, you must judge authors on how well they accomplish their purpose. In other words, you need to consider the type of passage (e.g., technical, persuasive, etc.) that the author has written and if the author has followed the requirements of the passage type.

> ➤ **Review Video: <u>Purpose of an Author</u>**
> *Visit **mometrix.com/academy** and enter **Code: 497555***

Writing Devices

Authors will use different stylistic and writing devices to make their meaning clear for readers. One of those devices is comparison and contrast. As mentioned previously, when an author describes the ways in which two things are alike, he or she is **comparing** them. When the author describes the ways in which two things are different, he or she is **contrasting** them. The "compare and contrast" essay is one of the most common forms in nonfiction. These passages are often signaled with certain words: a comparison may have indicating terms such as *both, same, like, too,* and *as well*; while a contrast may have terms like *but, however, on the other hand, instead,* and *yet*. Of course, comparisons and contrasts may be implicit without using any such signaling language. A single sentence may both compare and contrast. Consider the sentence *Brian and Sheila love ice cream, but Brian prefers vanilla and Sheila prefers strawberry.* In one sentence, the author has described both a similarity (love of ice cream) and a difference (favorite flavor).

> ➤ **Review Video: <u>Compare and Contrast</u>**
> *Visit **mometrix.com/academy** and enter **Code: 798319***

One of the most common text structures is **cause and effect**. A cause is an act or event that makes something happen, and an effect is the thing that happens as a result of the cause. A cause-and-effect relationship is not always explicit, but there are some terms in English that signal causes, such as *since, because,* and *due to*. Furthermore, terms that signal effects include *consequently, therefore, this lead(s) to.* As an example, consider the sentence *Because the sky was clear, Ron did not bring an umbrella.* The cause is the clear sky, and the effect is that Ron did not bring an umbrella. However, readers may find that sometimes the cause-and-effect relationship will not be clearly noted. For instance, the sentence *He was late and missed the meeting* does not contain any signaling words, but the sentence still contains a cause (he was late) and an effect (he missed the meeting).

Be aware of the possibility for a single cause to have multiple effects (e.g., *Single cause*: Because you left your homework on the table, your dog engulfs the assignment. *Multiple effects*: As a result, you receive a failing grade; your parents do not allow you to visit your friends; you miss out on the new movie and holding the hand of a potential significant other).

Also, the possibility of a single effect to have multiple causes (e.g.. *Single effect*: Alan has a fever. *Multiple causes*: An unexpected cold front came through the area, and Alan forgot to take his multi-vitamin to avoid being sick.)

Additionally, an effect can in turn be the cause of another effect, in what is known as a cause-and-effect chain. (e.g., As a result of her disdain for procrastination, Lynn prepared for her exam. This led to her passing her test with high marks. Hence, her resume was accepted and her application was approved.)

Authors often use analogies to add meaning to their passages. An **analogy** is a comparison of two things. The words in the analogy are connected by a certain, often undetermined relationship. Look at this analogy: *moo is to cow as quack is to duck*. This analogy compares the sound that a cow makes with the sound that a duck makes. Even if the word *quack* was not given, one could figure out the correct word to complete the analogy based on the relationship between the words *moo* and *cow*. Some common relationships for analogies include synonyms, antonyms, part to whole, definition, and actor to action.

Another element that impacts a text is the author's point-of-view. The **point of view** of a text is the perspective from which a passage is told. An author will always have a point of view about a story before he or she draws up a plot line. The author will know what events they want to take place, how they want the characters to interact, and how they want the story to resolve. An author will also have an opinion on the topic or series of events which is presented in the story that is based on their prior experience and beliefs.

The two main points of view that authors use--especially in a work of fiction--are first person and third person. If the narrator of the story is also the main character, or *protagonist*, the text is written in first-person point of view. In first person, the author writes from the perspective of *I*. Third-person point of view is probably the most common that authors use in their passages. Using third person, authors refer to each character by using *he* or *she*. In third-person omniscient, the narrator is not a character in the story and tells the story of all of the characters at the same time.

> ➤ **Review Video:** <u>Point of View</u>
> *Visit **mometrix.com/academy** and enter **Code: 383336**

Transitional words and phrases are devices that guide readers through a text. You are no doubt familiar with the common transitions, though you may never have considered how they operate. Some transitional phrases (*after, before, during, in the middle of*) give information about time. Some indicate that an example is about to be given (*for example, in* *fact, for instance*). Writers use them to compare (*also, likewise*) and contrast (*however, but, yet*). Transitional words and phrases can suggest addition (*and, also, furthermore, moreover*) and logical relationships (*if, then, therefore, as a result, since*). Finally, transitional words and phrases can separate the steps in a process (*first, second, last*).

> ➤ **Review Video:** <u>Transitional Words and Phrases</u>
> *Visit* ***mometrix.com/academy*** *and enter* ***Code:*** **197796**

Understanding a Passage

One of the most important skills in reading comprehension is the identification of **topics** and **main ideas.** There is a subtle difference between these two features. The topic is the subject of a text (i.e., what the text is all about). The main idea, on the other hand, is the most important point being made by the author. The topic is usually expressed in a few words at the most while the main idea often needs a full sentence to be completely defined. As an example, a short passage might have the topic of penguins and the main idea could be written as *Penguins are different from other birds in many ways.* In most nonfiction writing, the topic and the main idea will be stated directly and often appear in a sentence at the very beginning or end of the text. When being tested on an understanding of the author's topic, you may be able to skim the passage for the general idea, by reading only the first sentence of each paragraph. A body paragraph's first sentence is often--but not always--the main topic sentence which gives you a summary of the content in the paragraph.

However, there are cases in which the reader must figure out an unstated topic or main idea. In these instances, you must read every sentence of the text and try to come up with an overarching idea that is supported by each of those sentences.

Note: A thesis statement should not be confused with the main idea of the passage. While the main idea gives a brief, general summary of a text, the thesis statement provides a specific perspective on an issue that the author supports with evidence.

> ➤ **Review Video:** <u>Topics and Main Ideas</u>
> *Visit* ***mometrix.com/academy*** *and enter* ***Code:*** **691033**

Supporting details provide evidence and backing for the main point. In order to show that a main idea is correct, or valid, authors add details that prove their point. All texts contain details, but they are only classified as supporting details when they serve to reinforce some larger point. Supporting details are most commonly found in informative and persuasive texts. In some cases, they will be clearly indicated with terms like *for example* or *for instance*, or they will be enumerated with terms like *first*, *second*, and *last*. However, you need to be prepared for texts that do not contain those indicators. As a reader, you should consider whether the author's supporting details really back up his or her main point. Supporting details can be factual and correct, yet they may not be relevant to the author's point. Conversely, supporting details can seem pertinent, but they can be ineffective because they are based on opinion or assertions that cannot be proven.

> ➤ **Review Video:** <u>Supporting Details</u>
> Visit ***mometrix.com/academy*** and enter ***Code:* 396297**

An example of a main idea is: *Giraffes live in the Serengeti of Africa.* A supporting detail about giraffes could be: *A giraffe in this region benefits from a long neck by reaching twigs and leaves on tall trees.* The main idea gives the general idea that the text is about giraffes. The supporting detail gives a specific fact about how the giraffes eat.

As opposed to a main idea, themes are seldom expressed directly in a text and can be difficult to identify. A **theme** is an issue, an idea, or a question raised by the text. For instance, a theme of *Cinderella* (the Charles Perrault version) is perseverance as the title character serves her step-sisters and step-mother, and the prince seeks to find the girl with the missing slipper. A passage may have many themes, and you--as a dedicated reader--must take care to identify only themes that you are asked to find. One common characteristic of themes is that they raise more questions than they answer. In a good piece of fiction, authors are trying to elevate the reader's perspective and encourage him or her to consider the themes in a deeper way. In the process of reading, one can identify themes by constantly asking about the general issues that the text is addressing. A good way to evaluate an author's approach to a theme is to begin reading with a question in mind (e.g., How does this text approach the theme of love?) and to look for evidence in the text that addresses that question.

> ➤ **Review Video:** <u>Theme</u>
> Visit ***mometrix.com/academy*** and enter ***Code:* 732074**

Evaluating a Passage

When reading informational texts, there is importance in understanding the logical conclusion of the author's ideas. **Identifying a logical conclusion** can help you determine whether you agree with the writer or not. Coming to this conclusion is much like making an inference: the approach requires you to combine the information given by the text with what you already know in order to make a logical conclusion. If the author intended the reader to draw a certain conclusion, then you can expect the author's argumentation and detail to be leading in that direction. One way to approach the task of drawing conclusions is to make brief notes of all the points made by the author. When the notes are arranged on paper, they may clarify the logical conclusion. Another way to approach conclusions is to consider whether the reasoning of the author raises any pertinent questions. Sometimes you will be able to draw several conclusions from a passage. On occasion these will be conclusions that were never imagined by the author. Therefore, be aware that these conclusions must be supported directly by the text.

> **Review Video:** Identifying a Logical Conclusion
> *Visit **mometrix.com/academy** and enter **Code: 281653***

The term **text evidence** refers to information that supports a main point or minor points and can help lead the reader to a conclusion. Information used as text evidence is precise, descriptive, and factual. A main point is often followed by supporting details that provide evidence to back-up a claim. For example, a passage may include the claim that winter occurs during opposite months in the Northern and Southern hemispheres. Text evidence based on this claim may include countries where winter occurs in opposite months along with reasons that winter occurs at different times of the year in separate hemispheres (due to the tilt of the Earth as it rotates around the sun).

> **Review Video:** Text Evidence
> *Visit **mometrix.com/academy** and enter **Code: 486236***

A reader should always be drawing conclusions from the text. Sometimes conclusions are implied from written information, and other times the information is **stated directly** within the passage. One should always aim to draw conclusions from information stated within a passage, rather than to draw them from mere implications. At times an author may provide some information and then describe a counterargument. Readers should be alert for direct statements that are subsequently rejected or weakened by the author. Furthermore, you should always read through the entire passage before drawing conclusions. Many readers are trained to expect the author's conclusions at either the beginning or the end of the passage, but many texts do not adhere to this format.

Drawing conclusions from information implied within a passage requires confidence on the part of the reader. **Implications** are things that the author does not state directly, but readers can assume based on what the author does say. Consider the following passage: *I stepped outside and opened my umbrella. By the time I got to work, the cuffs of my pants were soaked*. The author never states that it is raining, but this fact is clearly implied. Conclusions based on implication must be well supported by the text. In order to draw a solid conclusion, readers should have multiple pieces of evidence. If readers have only one piece, they must be assured that there is no other possible explanation than their conclusion. A good reader will be able to draw many conclusions from information implied by the text which will be a great help in the exam.

As an aid to drawing conclusions, **outlining** the information contained in the passage should be a familiar skill to readers. An effective outline will reveal the structure of the passage and will lead to solid conclusions. An effective outline will have a title that refers to the basic subject of the text though the title needs not recapitulate the main idea. In most outlines, the main idea will be the first major section. Each major idea of the passage will be established as the head of a category. For instance, the most common outline format calls for the main ideas of the passage to be indicated with Roman numerals. In an effective outline of this kind, each of the main ideas will be represented by a Roman numeral and none of the Roman numerals will designate minor details or secondary ideas. Moreover, all supporting ideas and details should be placed in the appropriate place on the outline. An outline does not need to include every detail listed in the text, but the outline should feature all of those that are central to the argument or message. Each of these details should be listed under the appropriate main idea.

A helpful tool is the ability to **summarize** the information that you have read in a paragraph or passage format. This process is similar to creating an effective outline. First, a summary should accurately define the main idea of the passage though the summary does not need to explain this main idea in exhaustive detail. The summary should continue by laying out the most important supporting details or arguments from the passage. All of the significant supporting details should be included, and none of the details included should be irrelevant or insignificant. Also, the summary should accurately report all of these details. Too often, the desire for brevity in a summary leads to the sacrifice of clarity or accuracy. Summaries are often difficult to read because they omit all of the graceful language, digressions, and asides that distinguish great writing. However, an effective summary should contain much the same message as the original text.

Paraphrasing is another method that the reader can use to aid in comprehension. When paraphrasing, one puts what they have read into their words by rephrasing what the author has written, or one "translates" all of what the author shared into their words by including as many details as they can.

Responding to a Passage

When reading a good passage, readers are moved to engage actively in the text. One part of being an active reader involves making predictions. A **prediction** is a guess about what will happen next. Readers constantly make predictions based on what they have read and what they already know. Consider the following sentence: *Staring at the computer screen in shock, Kim blindly reached over for the brimming glass of water on the shelf to her side.* The sentence suggests that Kim is agitated, and that she is not looking at the glass that she is going to pick up. So, a reader might predict that Kim is going to knock over the glass. Of course, not every prediction will be accurate: perhaps Kim will pick the glass up cleanly. Nevertheless, the author has certainly created the expectation that the water might be spilled. Predictions are always subject to revision as the reader acquires more information.

> ➤ **Review Video: Predictions**
> Visit **mometrix.com/academy** and enter **Code: 437248**

Test-taking tip: To respond to questions requiring future predictions, your answers should be based on evidence of past or present behavior.

Readers are often required to understand a text that claims and suggests ideas without stating them directly. An **inference** is a piece of information that is implied but not written outright by the author. For instance, consider the following sentence: *After the final out of the inning, the fans were filled with joy and rushed the field*. From this sentence, a reader can infer that the fans were watching a baseball game and their team won the game. Readers should take great care to avoid using information beyond the provided passage before making inferences. As you practice with drawing inferences, you will find that they require concentration and attention.

> ➤ **Review Video:** <u>Inference</u>
> *Visit **mometrix.com/academy** and enter **Code:** 379203*

Test-taking tip: While being tested on your ability to make correct inferences, you must look for contextual clues. An answer can be *true* but not *correct*. The contextual clues will help you find the answer that is the best answer out of the given choices. Be careful in your reading to understand the context in which a phrase is stated. When asked for the implied meaning of a statement made in the passage, you should immediately locate the statement and read the context in which the statement was made. Also, look for an answer choice that has a similar phrase to the statement in question.

Readers must be able to identify a text's **sequence**, or the order in which things happen. Often, when the sequence is very important to the author, the text is indicated with signal words like *first*, *then*, *next*, and *last*. However, a sequence can be merely implied and must be noted by the reader. Consider the sentence *He walked through the garden and gave water and fertilizer to the plants*. Clearly, the man did not walk through the garden before he collected water and fertilizer for the plants. So, the implied sequence is that he first collected water, then he collected fertilizer, next he walked through the garden, and last he gave water or fertilizer as necessary to the plants. Texts do not always proceed in an orderly sequence from first to last. Sometimes they begin at the end and start over at the beginning. As a reader, you can enhance your understanding of the passage by taking brief notes to clarify the sequence.

In addition to inference and prediction, readers must often **draw conclusions** about the information they have read. When asked for a *conclusion* that may be drawn, look for critical "hedge" phrases, such as *likely*, *may*, *can*, *will often*, among many others. When you are being tested on this knowledge, remember the question that writers insert into these hedge phrases to cover every possibility. Often an answer will be wrong simply because there is no room for exception. Extreme positive or negative answers (such as always or never) are usually not correct. The reader <u>should not</u> use any outside knowledge that is not gathered from the passage to answer the related questions. Correct answers can be derived straight from the passage.

Cloze Test

A cloze test is a kind of reading test that measures how well you comprehend what you're reading, and also your ability to understand the context of what you're reading. It consists of a reading passage in which several words have been removed. In place of each removed word, there are a series of blank spaces indicating how many letters the removed word had. You must determine what word belongs in each set of blank spaces.

Review the following parts of speech to prepare for this sub-test of Reading Ability.

The Eight Parts of Speech

<u>Nouns</u>
When you talk about a person, place, thing, or idea, you are talking about nouns. The two main types of nouns are common and proper nouns. Also, nouns can be abstract (i.e., general) or concrete (i.e., specific).

Common nouns are the class or group of people, places, and things (Note: Do not capitalize common nouns). Examples of common nouns:
People: boy, girl, worker, manager
Places: school, bank, library, home
Things: dog, cat, truck, car

Proper nouns are the names of a specific person, place, or thing (Note: Capitalize all proper nouns). Examples of proper nouns:
People: Abraham Lincoln, George Washington, Martin Luther King, Jr.
Places: Los Angeles, California / New York / Asia
Things: Statue of Liberty, Earth*, Lincoln Memorial

*Note: When you talk about the planet that we live on, you capitalize *Earth*. When you mean the dirt, rocks, or land, you lowercase *earth*.

General nouns are the names of conditions or ideas. **Specific nouns** name people, places, and things that are understood by using your senses.

General nouns:
Condition: beauty, strength
Idea: truth, peace

Specific nouns:
People: baby, friend, father
Places: town, park, city hall
Things: rainbow, cough, apple, silk, gasoline

Collective nouns are the names for a person, place, or thing that may act as a whole. The following are examples of collective nouns: *class, company, dozen, group, herd, team,* and *public*.

Pronouns

Pronouns are words that are used to stand in for a noun. A pronoun may be grouped as personal, intensive, relative, interrogative, demonstrative, indefinite, and reciprocal.

Personal: Nominative is the case for nouns and pronouns that are the subject of a sentence. Objective is the case for nouns and pronouns that are an object in a sentence. Possessive is the case for nouns and pronouns that show possession or ownership.

Singular

	Nominative	Objective	Possessive
First Person	I	me	my, mine
Second Person	you	you	your, yours
Third Person	he, she, it	him, her, it	his, her, hers, its

Plural

	Nominative	Objective	Possessive
First Person	we	us	our, ours
Second Person	you	you	your, yours
Third Person	they	them	their, theirs

Intensive: I myself, you yourself, he himself, she herself, the (thing) itself, we ourselves, you yourselves, they themselves

Relative: which, who, whom, whose

Interrogative: what, which, who, whom, whose

Demonstrative: this, that, these, those

Indefinite: all, any, each, everyone, either/neither, one, some, several

Reciprocal: each other, one another

> ➢ **Review Video: Nouns and Pronouns**
> *Visit **mometrix.com/academy** and enter **Code: 312073***

Verbs

If you want to write a sentence, then you need a verb in your sentence. Without a verb, you have no sentence. The verb of a sentence explains action or being. In other words, the verb shows the subject's movement or the movement that has been done to the subject.

Transitive and Intransitive Verbs
A transitive verb is a verb whose action (e.g., drive, run, jump) points to a receiver (e.g., car, dog, kangaroo). Intransitive verbs do not point to a receiver of an action. In other words, the action of the verb does not point to a subject or object.

Transitive: He plays the piano. | The piano was played by him.

Intransitive: He plays. | John writes well.

A dictionary will let you know whether a verb is transitive or intransitive. Some verbs can be transitive and intransitive.

Action Verbs and Linking Verbs
An action verb is a verb that shows what the subject is doing in a sentence. In other words, an action verb shows action. A sentence can be complete with one word: an action verb. Linking verbs are intransitive verbs that show a condition (i.e., the subject is described but does no action).

Linking verbs link the subject of a sentence to a noun or pronoun, or they link a subject with an adjective. You always need a verb if you want a complete sentence. However, linking verbs are not able to complete a sentence.

Common linking verbs include *appear, be, become, feel, grow, look, seem, smell, sound,* and *taste*. However, any verb that shows a condition and has a noun, pronoun, or adjective that describes the subject of a sentence is a linking verb.

Action: He sings. | Run! | Go! | I talk with him every day. | She reads.

Linking:
Incorrect: I am.
Correct: I am John. | I smell roses. | I feel tired.

Note: Some verbs are followed by words that look like prepositions, but they are a part of the verb and a part of the verb's meaning. These are known as phrasal verbs and examples include *call off, look up*, and *drop off*.

Voice
Transitive verbs come in active or passive voice. If the subject does an action or receives the action of the verb, then you will know whether a verb is active or passive. When the subject of the sentence is doing the action, the verb is active voice. When the subject receives the action, the verb is passive voice.

Active: Jon drew the picture. (The subject *Jon* is doing the action of *drawing a picture*.)

Passive: The picture is drawn by Jon. (The subject *picture* is receiving the action from Jon.)

Verb Tenses

A verb tense shows the different form of a verb to point to the time of an action. The present and past tense are shown by changing the verb's form. An action in the present *I talk* can change form for the past: *I talked*. However, for the other tenses, an auxiliary (i.e., helping) verb is needed to show the change in form. These helping verbs include *am, are, is | have, has, had | was, were, will* (or *shall*).

Present: I talk   Present perfect: I have talked
Past: I talked   Past perfect: I had talked
Future: I will talk   Future perfect: I will have talked

Present: The action happens at the current time.
Example: He *walks* to the store every morning.
To show that something is happening right now, use the progressive present tense: I *am walking*.

Past: The action happened in the past.
Example: He *walked* to the store an hour ago.

Future: The action is going to happen later.
Example: I *will walk* to the store tomorrow.

Present perfect: The action started in the past and continues into the present.
Example: I *have walked* to the store three times today.

Past perfect: The second action happened in the past. The first action came before the second.
Example: Before I walked to the store (Action 2), I *had walked* to the library (Action 1).

Future perfect: An action that uses the past and the future. In other words, the action is complete before a future moment.
Example: When she comes for the supplies (future moment), I *will have walked* to the store (action completed in the past).

Conjugating Verbs

When you need to change the form of a verb, you are conjugating a verb. The key parts of a verb are first person singular, present tense (dream); first person singular, past tense (dreamed); and the past participle (dreamed). Note: the past participle needs a helping verb to make a verb tense. For example, I *have dreamed* of this day. | I *am dreaming* of this day.

Present Tense: Active Voice

	Singular	Plural
First Person	I dream	We dream
Second Person	You dream	You dream
Third Person	He, she, it dreams	They dream

Mood

There are three moods in English: the indicative, the imperative, and the subjunctive.

The **indicative mood** is used for facts, opinions, and questions.
Fact: You can do this.
Opinion: I think that you can do this.
Question: Do you know that you can do this?

The **imperative** is used for orders or requests.
Order: You are going to do this!
Request: Will you do this for me?

The **subjunctive mood** is for wishes and statements that go against fact.
Wish: I wish that I were going to do this.
Statement against fact: If I were you, I would do this. (This goes against fact because I am not you. You have the chance to do this, and I do not have the chance.)

The mood that causes trouble for most people is the subjunctive mood. If you have trouble with any of the moods, then be sure to practice.

Adjectives

An adjective is a word that is used to modify a noun or pronoun. An adjective answers a question: *Which one?*, *What kind of?*, or *How many?* . Usually, adjectives come before the words that they modify.

Which one?: The *third* suit is my favorite.
What kind?: The *navy blue* suit is my favorite.
How many?: Can I look over the *four* neckties for the suit?

Articles

Articles are adjectives that are used to mark nouns. There are only three: the definite (i.e., limited or fixed amount) article *the*, and the indefinite (i.e., no limit or fixed amount) articles *a* and *an*. Note: *An* comes before words that start with a vowel sound (i.e., vowels include *a, e, i, o, u,* and *y*). For example, Are you going to get an **u**mbrella?

Definite: I lost *the* bottle that belongs to me.
Indefinite: Does anyone have *a* bottle to share?

Comparison with Adjectives
Some adjectives are relative and other adjectives are absolute. Adjectives that are relative can show the comparison between things. Adjectives that are absolute can show comparison. However, they show comparison in a different way. Let's say that you are reading two books. You think that one book is perfect, and the other book is not exactly perfect. It is <u>not</u> possible for the book to be more perfect than the other. Either you think that the book is perfect, or you think that the book is not perfect.

The adjectives that are relative will show the different degrees of something or someone to something else or someone else. The three degrees of adjectives include positive, comparative, and superlative.

The positive degree is the normal form of an adjective.
Example: This work is *difficult*. | She is *smart*.

The comparative degree compares one person or thing to another person or thing.
Example: This work is *more difficult* than your work. | She is *smarter* than me.

The superlative degree compares more than two people or things.
Example: This is the *most difficult* work of my life. | She is the *smartest* lady in school.

➢ **Review Video: <u>What is an Adjective?</u>**
*Visit **mometrix.com/academy** and enter **Code:** **470154***

Adverbs
An adverb is a word that is used to modify a verb, adjective, or another adverb. Usually, adverbs answer one of these questions: *When?, Where?, How?,* and *Why?* . The negatives *not* and *never* are known as adverbs. Adverbs that modify adjectives or other adverbs strengthen or weaken the words that they modify.

Examples:
He walks quickly through the crowd.
The water flows smoothly on the rocks.

Note: While many adverbs end in *-ly*, you need to remember that not all adverbs end in *-ly*. Also, some words that end in *-ly* are adjectives, not adverbs. Some examples include: *early, friendly, holy, lonely, silly,* and *ugly*. To know if a word that ends in *-ly* is an adjective or adverb, you need to check your dictionary.

Examples:

He is *never* angry.

You talk *too* loud.

Comparison with Adverbs

The rules for comparing adverbs are the same as the rules for adjectives.

The positive degree is the standard form of an adverb.

Example: He arrives soon. | She speaks softly to her friends.

The comparative degree compares one person or thing to another person or thing.

Example: He arrives sooner than Sarah. | She speaks more softly than him.

The superlative degree compares more than two people or things.

Example: He arrives soonest of the group. | She speaks most softly of any of her friends.

> ➤ **Review Video: Adverbs**
> Visit **mometrix.com/academy** and enter **Code: 713951**

Prepositions

A preposition is a word placed before a noun or pronoun that shows the relationship between an object and another word in the sentence.

Common prepositions:

about	before	during	on	under
after	beneath	for	over	until
against	between	from	past	up
among	beyond	in	through	with
around	by	of	to	within
at	down	off	toward	without

Examples:

The napkin is *in* the drawer.

The Earth rotates *around* the Sun.

The needle is *beneath* the haystack.

Can you find me *among* the words?

> ➤ **Review Video: What is a Preposition?**
> Visit **mometrix.com/academy** and enter **Code: 946763**

Conjunctions

Conjunctions join words, phrases, or clauses, and they show the connection between the joined pieces. There are coordinating conjunctions that connect equal parts of sentences. Correlative conjunctions show the connection between pairs. Subordinating conjunctions join subordinate (i.e., dependent) clauses with independent clauses.

Coordinating Conjunctions

The coordinating conjunctions include: *and, but, yet, or, nor, for,* and *so*
Examples:
The rock was small, but it was heavy.
She drove in the night, and he drove in the day.

Correlative Conjunctions

The correlative conjunctions are: *either...or* | *neither...nor* | *not only... but also*
Examples:
Either you are coming, *or* you are staying. | He ran *not only* three miles, *but also* swam 200 yards.

> ➤ **Review Video: Coordinating and Correlative Conjunctions**
> *Visit* ***mometrix.com/academy*** *and enter* ***Code: 390329***

Subordinating Conjunctions

Common subordinating conjunctions include:

after	since	whenever
although	so that	where
because	unless	wherever
before	until	whether
in order that	when	while

Examples:
I am hungry *because* I did not eat breakfast.
He went home *when* everyone left.

> ➤ **Review Video: Subordinating Conjunctions**
> *Visit* ***mometrix.com/academy*** *and enter* ***Code: 958913***

Interjections

An interjection is a word for exclamation (i.e., great amount of feeling) that is used alone or as a piece to a sentence. Often, they are used at the beginning of a sentence for an introduction. Sometimes, they can be used in the middle of a sentence to show a change in thought or attitude.

Common Interjections: Hey! | Oh,... | Ouch! | Please! | Wow!

Examples

You will need to use contextual clues to complete the sentences with the missing words. One strategy you may use is substitution. A good reader will brainstorm some possible words for the blank space, and he or she will substitute these words into the sentence. If the sentence and the surrounding passage continue to make sense, then the substitution has revealed the missing word. Be sure that the word you use occupies every provided space for a letter. If there are six blank spaces for the missing word, then you need a word with six letters.

Example 1
The father ran to help the _ _ _ _ _ on the bike.

In this example, we see the connection between a father and someone riding a bike. You can tell from this example that the missing word is a noun that has five letters. To select a word for the blank, you need to think about the context of the sentence. A father is running to take care of someone on the bike. So, one possible choice is child. A father is teaching his child to ride a bike, and the child needs assistance. Another possible choice is woman. There are five letters in the word, and it makes sense at least in this sentence. To know which word to choose, you would need to focus on the whole paragraph that will be provided to you. Be sure that you don't focus only on the blank spaces to fill in with the correct number of letters. Take time to read the whole paragraph and think about the context.

Example 2
The soldiers saluted their commander as _ _ _ entered the room.

In this example, we see the connection between soldiers and their commanding officer. You can tell from this example that the missing word is a pronoun that refers to the commander, not the soldiers. We know that there is only one commander because there is no plural "s" to show more than one. So, we are looking for a singular, third-person, personal pronoun that refers to a man or woman: *he* or *she*. Now, you can tell from the dashes that the missing word has three letters. So, you know that your answer is *she*.

Reasoning Ability

Reasoning

The reasoning sub-test uses the format of multiple choice questions to determine if you will be able to understand a logical sequence of ideas. Most questions fall into a few categories. However, each question will present you with a set of information, expect you to determine patterns, and ask for information based on those patterns.

Comparative Values

In this type of problem, you will be given a few comparisons between people or objects. The question will ask you to order the people or objects from least to greatest or find the value of specific person or object. The key to these problems is to create a hierarchy based on the provided relationships.

Example:

Oak, Pecan, Evergreen, and Maple trees are rated by popularity in neighborhoods. Oak ranks in between Maple and Pecan. Maple ranks higher than Pecan. Evergreen is rated lowest. Which tree is rated highest?

a. Pecan
b. Oak
c. Evergreen
d. Maple

The answer is D. Maple. Starting with the lowest of Evergreen, the next highly rated tree will be Pecan because Oak separates the other two, of which pecan is lower. Oak is lower than Maple. Maple is the highest rated tree.

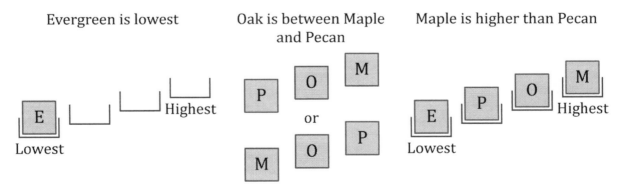

Numerical Series

In this type of problem, you will be given a set of numbers in a specific order. The question will ask you to find the value of the next number. The key to these problems is to check for constant increase/decrease, which could indicate adding or multiplying each number by another number, or check for repetition.

Example:

Identify the next number in the series: 5, 4, 3, 5, 4…
    a. 2
    b. 3
    c. 4
    d. 5

The answer is B. 3. Although the first three numbers seem to be decreasing by one each position, the fourth number restarts the process. Thus, the numbers are repeating. The number after 4 will be 3.

Similar Words

In this type of problem, you will be given a set of words, three of which are similar. The question will ask you to find which word is different from the others. The key to these problems is to check for commonalities between the words and pick the word that doesn't fit.

Three of the following words are similar, while one is different. Select the one that is different.
    a. bike
    b. scooter
    c. flying
    d. skateboard

The answer is C. flying. Although all words have to do with transportation, flying is the only word which isn't a vehicle.

Practice Test #1

Clarity

Instructions: In the following pairs of sentences, identify the sentence that is most clearly written. If sentence "a" is more clear than sentence "b," mark "a" on your answer sheet. If sentence "b" is more clear than sentence "a," mark "b" on your answer sheet.

1.   a. The recidivism rate for older criminals was much higher than for younger criminals.
b. The recidivism rate for older criminals was much higher than younger.

2.   a. Denise remembered with a start. That she had forgotten to lock the car.
b. Denise remembered with a start that she had forgotten to lock the car.

3.   a. The officers were involved in bringing the case to a successful conclusion.
b. The officers brought the case to a successful conclusion.

4.   a. Officers and civilians occasionally come into conflict with one another; this could be avoided if they talked to them more.
b. Officers and civilians occasionally come into conflict with one another; this could be avoided if officers talked to civilians more.

5.   a. At the age of seventeen, Dave's teacher told him that he should consider medical school.
b. When Dave was seventeen, his teacher told him that he should consider medical school.

6.   a. Every February he did the same thing: renewed his library card.
b. Every February he did the same thing, renewed his library card.

7.   a. Leaders should get used to being criticized when they are wrong and ignored when they are right.
b. A leader should get used to being criticized when they are wrong and ignored when they are right.

8.   a. Throughout the interrogation, Calvin denied that the assailant was he.
b. Calvin denied throughout the interrogation that he was the assailant.

9.   a. Living near a power station can be unhealthy; it is associated with higher rates of cancer.
b. Living near a power substation can be unhealthy, it is associated with higher rates of cancer.

10.	a. Being a police officer involves a great deal of lifting weights and paperwork.
b. Being a police officer involves a great deal of lifting weights and filling out paperwork.

11.	a. You need to have a driver's license, a second form of identification, and a signed waiver to enter.
b. One needs a driver's license and a second form of identification to enter, and you have to sign a waiver as well.

12.	a. The house, which was set at the back of the property, had a number of outbuildings, including a shed.
b. The house which was set at the back of the property had a number of outbuildings including a shed.

13.	a. After reading the manual again, the inner workings of the engine made much more sense to Linda.
b. The inner workings of the engine made much more sense to Linda after she read the manual again.

14.	a. Dr. Gerard worked at the precinct station as a staff psychologist.
b. Dr. Gerard was employed at the precinct station working as a staff psychologist.

15.	a. When entering the house, the smell of almonds aroused Kevin's suspicion.
b. Kevin's suspicion was aroused by the smell of almonds as he entered the house.

Spelling

Instructions: In the following sentences, choose the correct spelling of the missing word. Mark on your answer sheet the letter that identifies the correct choice.

16. "That is your fifth _____ this month," the teacher remarked sternly.
    a. abscence
    b. absence
    c. abscess
    d. absense

17. By the time the clock chimed for the _____ time, Peter was already up the stairs and in his room.
    a. twelth
    b. twelfth
    c. twelf
    d. twelvth

18. Whenever she was in that part of town, she liked to stop by and visit the _____ where her mother was buried.
    a. cematery
    b. cematary
    c. semetary
    d. cemetery

19. His soothing words and manner were able to calm even the most _____ dog.
    a. vishus
    b. vicous
    c. viciouss
    d. vicious

20. No matter how hard he tried, he could never master the _____ of the difficult piano composition.
    a. rithm
    b. rhythm
    c. rhthm
    d. rythm

21. Denise spent her Saturday mornings picking up garbage, clothes, and other _____ debris that collected along the shore by her house.
    a. misselaneous
    b. miscellaneous
    c. miselanious
    d. misselanneous

22. An effective public servant must always be _____ of the needs and desires of the community.
    a. conscious
    b. conchess
    c. consious
    d. conscience

23. The car dealership was giving away _____ replicas of its most popular sports car as a sales promotion.
    a. minature
    b. minercher
    c. miniature
    d. minacher

24. Leonard reminded the hotel clerk that he would need a _____ for his expense account.
    a. reseet
    b. reseat
    c. receipt
    d. receit

25. The court gave permission for the state to _____ all of Mr. Davis' assets after his felony conviction.
    a. seize
    b. seez
    c. cease
    d. seaz

26. The cafe's employees were instructed that hand washing should _____ any contact with food or areas where food would be prepared.
    a. proceed
    b. precede
    c. preceed
    d. preseed

27. Sloan locked her car door more frequently after hearing that there was a _____ in the neighborhood.
    a. berglur
    b. burglur
    c. burglar
    d. burgler

28. Felicia attributed the _____ noise she had heard in the night to a fight between the neighborhood cats.
    a. weird
    b. weerd
    c. wierd
    d. weyrd

29. Fred hoped he could one day be promoted all the way to _____, just as his father and grandfather had before him.
    a. sergeant
    b. sargent
    c. sergent
    d. sargeant

30. Not every state facility is able to provide _____ accommodations for males and females.
    a. seperate
    b. separate
    c. saparate
    d. sepperate

Vocabulary

Instructions: In each of the following sentences, choose the word or phrase that most nearly has the same meaning as the underlined word. Mark on your answer sheet the letter that identifies the correct choice.

31. Only his <u>tenacious</u> grip enabled him to hang onto the sheer cliff face.
    a. lively
    b. fragile
    c. persistent
    d. complicated

32. The story seemed <u>credible</u>, but the investigators still needed to follow up on it.
    a. amazing
    b. believable
    c. dirty
    d. crumbly

33. Only the most <u>partisan</u> supporters of the team believed the coach's story.
    a. ignorant
    b. uninterested
    c. festive
    d. supporter

34. The <u>premise</u> of the movie was that time travel had become common and affordable.
    a. argument
    b. conclusion
    c. decision
    d. thought

35. A police officer who excels at her job may receive an <u>accolade</u> from the local media.
    a. drama
    b. compliment
    c. feature
    d. deadline

36. He seemed to be in <u>perpetual</u> motion without ever getting anything done.
    a. timed
    b. mobile
    c. continuous
    d. inconstant

37. An administrative oversight made it necessary for him to <u>rescind</u> the original oversight.
    a. invalidate
    b. put back
    c. create
    d. allege

38. He installed a solar panel so that he could <u>generate</u> some of his own electricity.
    a. annoy
    b. select
    c. enjoy
    d. produce

39. Sometimes even the most <u>incompatible</u> partners can complete some excellent work.
    a. agreeable
    b. conflicting
    c. friendly
    d. compliant

40. His material <u>prosperity</u> did not compensate for the personal losses he had suffered.
    a. penury
    b. possibility
    c. wealth
    d. deadliness

41. Gina was a <u>novice</u> but she still performed rather well.
    a. newcomer
    b. veteran
    c. senior
    d. speculator

42. He spoke with <u>candor</u> despite his love for the men.
    a. relevance
    b. frankness
    c. strategy
    d. gratitude

43. He tried to be <u>prudent</u> with his money, but he still ended up broke at the end of every month.
    a. aware
    b. calm
    c. standard
    d. cautious

44. Since Fred was young, he had had an <u>innate</u> ability to make other people feel comfortable.
    a. inherent
    b. intense
    c. slick
    d. prepared

45. His parents had taught him to act <u>submissive</u> and calm if he ever encountered a bear in the woods.
    a. creative
    b. passive
    c. underwater
    d. aggressive

Reading Comprehension

Instructions: Officers must read and understand a wide range of materials. This test is designed to measure your ability to read and understand various types of written material. Read each paragraph or passage and choose the statement that best answers the question. All questions pertain only to the material in the passage that precedes them. Choose your answer solely on the basis of the material contained in the passage. Mark the letter that identifies your choice in the space on your answer sheet. Do not spend too much time on any one item.

Questions 46 and 47 are based on the following passage:

> Randy Barron was excited to apply for a marriage license in Washington County, but he was soon met with obstacles. After Mr. Barron got through the front door of the county building, he found that the ramp going down to the Recorder of Deeds office was too steep for him to safely use his wheelchair. Additionally, there was insufficient room for him to maneuver his wheelchair to a flat surface to reach the door to the office. Barriers to accessibility mean that people like Mr. Barron will not be able to fully benefit from services and programs, including experiencing the happiest of moments of our lives, like applying for a marriage license.

46. Based on the preceding passage, which of the following statements is most accurate?
    a. Randy Barron could not fit his wheelchair through the front door of the county building.
    b. The door to the county building was locked, so Randy Barron could not enter.
    c. Randy Barron could not navigate his wheelchair down a steep ramp.
    d. Randy Barron could not push his wheelchair up a steep ramp.

47. Based on the preceding passage, which of the following statements is most accurate?
    a. Randy Barron's acquisition of a marriage license was made more difficult by barriers to accessibility.
    b. Randy Barron could not get married because of barriers to accessibility.
    c. Handicapped people cannot get married in Washington County.
    d. The Recorder of Deeds should switch offices with another county employee.

Questions 48 and 49 are based on the following passage:

When 911 or other call takers receive a request for service that they suspect involves a person with a mental illness, they should gather descriptive information on the person's behavior; determine whether the individual appears to pose a danger to himself, herself, or others; ascertain whether the person possesses or has access to weapons; and ask the caller about the person's history of mental health or substance abuse treatment, violence, or victimization. All call takers should receive training on how to collect the most useful information quickly. To supplement this training, members of the coordinating group with mental health backgrounds should develop a concise list of questions for call takers to have on hand when answering service requests that seem to involve someone with a mental illness.

48. Based on the preceding passage, which of the following statements is most accurate?
    a. A 911 dispatcher is not allowed to inquire about a person's history of mental illness.
    b. The mentally ill should receive the same treatment as everyone else from 911 dispatchers.
    c. The list of questions for cases involving mental illness should be drafted with input from call takers.
    d. There are special concerns for a 911 dispatcher when dealing with the mentally ill.

49. Based on the preceding passage, which of the following statements is most accurate?
    a. A 911 operator usually gets a second chance to acquire key information.
    b. It is important for 911 dispatchers to collect information quickly.
    c. The mentally ill have the same access to weapons as other citizens.
    d. Not every 911 call taker needs to receive training for dealing with the mentally ill.

Questions 50 and 51 are based on the following passage:

Police officers sometimes need to control violent, combative people. Their actions under such circumstances are governed by use-of-force protocols. Less-lethal technologies give police an alternative to using other physical force options that potentially are more dangerous to officers and suspects. The technologies currently in use include conducted-energy devices (such as Tasers), beanbag rounds, pepper spray, and stun grenades. When deciding to use less-lethal equipment, officers consider the circumstances and their agency's policy. Almost all larger law enforcement agencies have written policies about the use of less-lethal force. As part of their policy, agencies often have an approved use-of-force continuum to help officers decide the suitable amount of force for a situation — higher levels of force in the most severe circumstances, and less force in other circumstances. Many agencies in which officers use less-lethal technologies have training programs to help evaluate dangerous circumstances.

50. Based on the preceding passage, which of the following statements is most accurate?
   a. Only a few large law enforcement agencies have written policies about the use of less-lethal force.
   b. The use of less-lethal technologies reduces the danger for officers.
   c. Officers are typically required to use the maximum amount of force whenever possible.
   d. Stun grenades are not considered a less-lethal technology.

51. Based on the preceding passage, which of the following statements is most accurate?
   a. Less-lethal technology is appropriate for any situation.
   b. Officers must use their own judgment when assessing danger.
   c. Less-lethal technology is an alternative to rather than a replacement for traditional physical force methods.
   d. Stun grenades are an example of a conducted-energy device.

Questions 52 and 53 are based on the information listed below:
   Radio code is the coding system for identifying units both inside and outside the department. There are three components to every radio code. Each of these components must be included when officers are dispatched. In this coding system, units are identified with three characters: a letter designating the shift, a number designating the operational assignment, and a number identifying the area.

   Shift
   A: Day
   B: Swing
   C: Graveyard

   Operational assignment
   1: Traffic division, motorcycle
   2: Traffic division, horse
   3: Traffic division, bicycle
   4: Patrol division, platoon 1
   5: Patrol division, platoon 2
   6: Investigation division, drugs
   7: Investigation division, financial crime
   8: Investigation division, homicide
   9: Administration division

   Area
   1-9: North side
   10-15: East side
   16-22: West side
   23-29: South side
   30-34: Downtown

52. Using the above coding system, the call number A-3-8 would identify:
    a. day; traffic division, bicycle; north side
    b. swing; traffic division, horse; west side
    c. swing; investigation division, financial crime; east side
    d. graveyard; traffic division, horse; downtown

53. Using the above coding system, the call number C-4-33 would identify:
    a. day; patrol division, platoon 1; south side
    b. graveyard; traffic division, bicycle; west side
    c. graveyard; patrol division, platoon 1; downtown
    d. swing; traffic division, horse; south side

Questions 54 and 55 are based on the following passage:

Visibility is essential to roadside safety for emergency responders. Can drivers see and recognize an emergency vehicle as it navigates through traffic on its way to the scene of an accident or fire? When the first responder has reached the scene and is on the side of the road, can drivers clearly see both the person and the vehicle?

Several factors affect a vehicle's visibility — its size and color, for example. Environmental conditions, such as the weather and time of day, also play a role in whether drivers can easily see emergency vehicles along the road.

Emergency vehicles have features designed to draw attention to their presence even when drivers are not actively looking for them. These include warning lights, sirens and horns, and retro-reflective striping, which reflects light back to its source. Such features provide information about the vehicle's size, position, speed, and direction of travel so drivers can take suitable action.

54. Based on the preceding passage, which of the following statements is most accurate?
    a. It is more important for an emergency vehicle to be visible when it is in motion.
    b. Emergency vehicle sirens help improve their visibility.
    c. The weather and the time of day are the only environmental conditions that affect a vehicle's visibility.
    d. Emergency vehicles are always painted in special colors to improve their visibility.

55. Based on the preceding passage, which of the following statements is most accurate?
    a. Emergency responders must be visible when in motion and when stopped.
    b. Only emergency vehicles have features that provide information to other drivers.
    c. Retro-reflective lighting is useless during the day.
    d. Other drivers only need to know the location of an emergency responder in order to respond correctly.

Question 56 is based on the following passage:

As a Buffalo, NY parking meter mechanic, James Bagarozzo was supposed to service and repair the city's 1,200 mechanical machines, but he didn't have access to their coin canisters and was not authorized to collect money. Instead, he rigged the meters so that deposited quarters never dropped into the coin canisters. Then he retrieved the money for himself. Beginning in 2003 and continuing until the time of his arrest years later, the 57-year-old stole thousands upon thousands of quarters, using bags in his car or his deep-pocketed work pants to transfer the loot to his home, where he rolled the change in coin wrappers and exchanged it for cash at the bank.

56. Based on the preceding passage, which of the following statements is most accurate?
    a. James Bagarozzo was responsible for collecting the money from parking meters in Buffalo.
    b. James Bagarozzo had a criminal history before he began working as a parking meter mechanic.
    c. Bagarozzo deposited the stolen money into his bank account.
    d. In Buffalo, parking meter mechanics do not have access to the coin canisters.

Questions 57 and 58 are based on the following passage:

In a sample of police departments surveyed in 2013, approximately 75 percent of them reported that they did not use body-worn cameras. A report about the survey notes a number of perceived benefits for using body-worn cameras, including better evidence documentation and increased accountability and transparency. But the report also notes many other factors that law enforcement executives must consider, such as privacy issues, officer and community concerns, data retention and public disclosure policies, and financial considerations. The costs of implementing body-worn cameras include not only the cost of the cameras, but also of any ancillary equipment (e.g., tablets that let officers tag data in the field), data storage and management, training, administration, and disclosure. To date, little research is available to help law enforcement executives decide whether and how to implement the use of body-worn cameras in their departments.

57. Based on the preceding passage, which of the following statements is most accurate?
    a. Most police departments do not use body-worn cameras.
    b. There are no disadvantages to the use of body-worn cameras.
    c. Body-worn cameras are inexpensive.
    d. Body-worn cameras make police officers transparent.

58. Based on the preceding passage, which of the following statements is most accurate?
    a. Body-worn cameras are not right for every police department.
    b. There is a large body of research on the use of body-worn cameras.
    c. Most police officers prefer not to wear cameras.
    d. Body-worn cameras are difficult to operate.

Question 59 is based on the following passage:

Fire and arson investigators examine the physical attributes of a fire scene and identify and collect physical evidence from the scene. This evidence is then analyzed to help determine if the cause of the fire was accidental or deliberate. During the scene examination, investigators may find evidence such as accelerants, tampered utilities, and specific burn patterns, which may indicate criminal activity.

59. Based on the preceding passage, which of the following statements is most accurate?
    a. Burn patterns indicate criminal activity.
    b. Arson investigators do not always find evidence of criminal activity at a fire scene.
    c. Arson investigators question suspects and try to establish motive.
    d. Arson investigators are responsible for analyzing the physical evidence collected at the scene.

Question 60 is based on the following passage:

Suspects in cars who flee from law enforcement place themselves, the officers, and bystanders in hazardous situations. High-speed pursuits often result in property damage and may result in injury or death. About half of all high-speed pursuits last less than two minutes and most last less than six minutes. Officers must act instantly, weighing the need to protect public safety against the need to apprehend fleeing suspects.

60. Based on the preceding passage, which of the following statements is most accurate?
    a. High-speed pursuits cause more injuries than deaths.
    b. High-speed pursuits require officers to make the right decision in an instant.
    c. Most high-speed pursuits are longer than six minutes.
    d. High-speed pursuits are the largest cause of officer fatalities.

Question 61 is based on the following passage:

Law enforcement officers often use conducted-energy devices (CEDs) to get noncompliant or hostile suspects to comply. CEDs, such as Tasers, induce involuntary muscle contractions, causing the suspect to be temporarily incapacitated. CEDs are controversial because of safety concerns. The concerns are not solely with the technology itself but with the policies and training for using the devices. Clearly defined policies and thorough training are needed to ensure that any use-of-force technique is used only when necessary to protect officers, suspects, and bystanders. When CEDs are properly used as an alternative to deadly force, they can help reduce injuries to officers and suspects alike.

61. Based on the preceding passage, which of the following statements is most accurate?
   a. CEDs are a totally safe alternative to conventional methods of force.
   b. CEDs are not totally safe, but they are safer than conventional methods of force.
   c. Most police departments provide extensive training related to the use of conducted-energy devices.
   d. Tasers are not an example of a conducted-energy device.

Questions 62 and 63 are based on the following passage:

There is a specific protocol for classifying crimes, and law enforcement officers are required to follow this protocol at all times. Victimizations and incidents are classified based on detailed characteristics of the event provided by the respondent. Neither victims nor interviewers classify crimes at the time of interview. During data processing, a computer program classifies each event into one type of crime, based on the entries on a number of items on the survey questionnaire. This ensures that similar events will be classified using a standard procedure. The glossary definition for each crime indicates the major characteristics required to be so classified. If an event can be classified as more than one type of crime, a hierarchy is used that classifies the crime according to the most serious event that occurred. The hierarchy is: rape, sexual assault, robbery, assault, burglary, motor vehicle theft, theft.

62. Based on the preceding passage, which of the following statements is most accurate?
   a. Crimes are not classified while victims are being interviewed.
   b. The crime classification system only needs to be observed occasionally.
   c. Crime classification is based on the first offense reported by the victim.
   d. Police officers have control over the items on the survey questionnaire.

63. Based on the preceding passage, which of the following statements is most accurate?
   a. Theft is a more serious crime than robbery.
   b. Motor vehicle theft is a more serious crime than assault.
   c. Sexual assault is a more serious crime than motor vehicle theft.
   d. Assault is a more serious crime than robbery.

Questions 64 and 65 are based on the following passage:

There are some easy ways for employers to reduce employee theft. Employees who are treated fairly and generously are less likely to steal. Get to know your employees. Ask for their suggestions and seriously consider them. Involve employees in crime prevention practices. Consider starting a profit-sharing program. Make sure your salary rates are competitive — an underpaid employee may feel that stealing from you merely "makes up the difference."

64. Based on the preceding passage, which of the following statements is most accurate?
   a. Strong relationships between owners and employees decrease the incidence of employee theft.
   b. Employees at thriving businesses are less likely to steal.
   c. Employees should lead crime prevention practices.
   d. Employee theft can be reduced by encouraging competition between employees.

65. Based on the preceding passage, which of the following statements is most accurate?
   a. Sometimes employees steal because they feel that they are underpaid.
   b. Employees should be paid as much as their employers.
   c. Businesses with profit-sharing programs always experience less employee theft.
   d. Employee theft is the most common crime in the workplace.

Cloze

It (66) _ _ _ _ a great deal of time and effort, but the Davis County Police Department (67) _ _ _ eventually able to catch a sophisticated jewel thief who had been breaking (68) _ _ _ _ expensive homes for at least two years. The evidence gathered (69) _ _ _ _ the criminal's hideout suggested that at least fifty homes in the area had (70) _ _ _ _ burglarized.

The burglaries began in March of 2008, (71) _ _ _ _ an elderly woman in the exclusive Haverford Heights subdivision reported that (72) _ _ antique pearl necklace had (73) _ _ _ _ stolen from her dresser while she was out of town. The evidence found (74) _ _ the woman's home would become very familiar to the detectives who worked on (75) _ _ _ _ case: a bathroom window had been forced (76) _ _ _ _ with a crowbar, and someone had crawled in. There (77) _ _ _ _ footprints in the dirt outside the window, but police found the shoes that made the (78) _ _ _ _ _ _ in a garbage can down the street. This (79) _ _ _ a trademark of the burglar: he or she always wore new (80) _ _ _ _ _, which were discarded immediately (81) _ _ _ _ _ the job was finished.

After the first burglary, (82) _ _ _ _ _ was a short period in which the criminal was inactive. However, two months later, he (83) _ _ she struck again: a set of diamond earrings was stolen (84) _ _ _ _ the home of a vacationing couple, (85) _ _ _ several precious stones were taken from an elderly woman. Each time, the (86) _ _ _ _ _ _ found a pair of new shoes in a nearby garbage can. Within the department, the detectives began referring to the (87) _ _ _ _ _ as "the Size Eleven Bandit." However, despite their best efforts, they could (88) _ _ _ make a break in the case.

The burglaries then increased in frequency, (89) _ _ _ _ seven occurring over the next three months. The police (90) _ _ _ _ _ tell that the criminal was becoming more brazen, but they still were unable to make any headway in the case. It was clear that the criminal was intelligent and patient, and (91) _ _ _ _ a great deal about precious stones. However, he or she was (92) _ _ _ _ very careful to avoid leaving behind any clues that would (93) _ _ _ _ the detectives.

The burglaries continued for more than a year. Several times, the police (94) _ _ _ _ sure that they had made a break in the case, but each of these leads dried up in the end. Finally, one of the detectives working on the case assembled a (95) _ _ _ _ of all the shoes found at the various crime scenes, and took this list around to all of the shoe stores (96) _ _ the area. It turned out that only one (97) _ _ _ _ _ sold all of the different types of shoes worn (98) _ _ the burglar during his or her crimes. The detective then examined the sales records of the store, and discovered (99) _ _ _ _ several of the shoes had been purchased (100) _ _ _ _ the same credit card, a (101) _ _ _ _ belonging to Kevin Fuller of Finley Station. A (102) _ _ _ _ _ _ of Fuller's home revealed a stash of stolen jewelry, and Fuller himself (103) _ _ _ apprehended later that week as (104) _ _ shopped for groceries. He immediately confessed (105) _ _ the burglaries.

Reasoning

Instructions: Officers often face situations in which they need to determine how different pieces of information relate to one another. In this section, you will be presented with information such as a group or ordered series of facts, numbers, letters, or words. Your task is to study the various pieces of information and try to understand how they relate to one another. Mark the letter that identifies your choice on your answer sheet.

106. Identify the next number in the series: 45, 42, 39, 36, 33...
     a. 29
     b. 35
     c. 32
     d. 30

107. In the three-legged race, Aaron finished after Bruce, but before Carl. In what order did the participants finish?
     a. Carl, Aaron, Bruce
     b. Aaron, Carl, Bruce
     c. Bruce, Aaron, Carl
     d. Carl, Bruce, Aaron

108. Three of the following words are similar, while one is different. Select the one that is different.
     a. ramp
     b. house
     c. castle
     d. shack

109. Identify the next number in the series: 12, 27, 36, 12, 27, 36, 12...
     a. 12
     b. 27
     c. 36
     d. 49

110. Ellen, Fiona, Gretchen, and Helen were in a race. Ellen finished ahead of Gretchen, and the other two girls tied. Who came in second place?
     a. Ellen
     b. Gretchen
     c. Helen
     d. Not enough information

111. On their last Spanish test, Dave received a 92 and scored ten points better than Edgar. However, Edgar scored four points better than Philip, who scored three points better than Quincy. What was Philip's score?
    a. 75
    b. 78
    c. 82
    d. 85

112. Identify the next number in the series: 1, 2, 5, 10, 17, 26…
    a. 35
    b. 37
    c. 38
    d. 40

113. Frank weighs more than George, and George weighs less than Henry. Who weighs the most?
    a. Frank
    b. George
    c. Henry
    d. Not enough information

114. Three of the following words are similar, while one is different. Select the one that is different.
    a. fierce
    b. container
    c. quiet
    d. grainy

115. Identify the next number in the series: 39, 32, 31, 24, 23, 16…
    a. 9
    b. 10
    c. 15
    d. 16

116. Three of the following words are similar, while one is different. Select the one that is different.
    a. milk
    b. banana
    c. juice
    d. soda

117. Identify the next number in the series: 1, 2, 4, 7, 11, 16…
    a. 20
    b. 21
    c. 22
    d. 24

118. Xavier, Yolanda, and Zeke are in a race. Zeke finishes ahead of Yolanda but behind Xavier. Who finished in last place?
    a. Xavier
    b. Yolanda
    c. Zeke
    d. Not enough information

119. Identify the next number in the series: 37, 32, 37, 32...
    a. 32
    b. 35
    c. 37
    d. Not enough information

120. Three of the following words are similar, while one is different. Select the one that is different.
    a. planet
    b. remote control
    c. coat
    d. elevator

121. Identify the next number in the series: 8, 14, 9, 15, 10, 16...
    a. 10
    b. 11
    c. 17
    d. 18

Answers and Explanations #1

Clarity

1. A: In the other version, the comparison being made is not clear. The correct version of the sentence makes it clear that the comparison is with younger criminals, and not just the generally younger. Including the word criminal at the end of the sentence makes the comparison clear.

2. B: The other version is a sentence and a sentence fragment. The expression "That she had forgotten to lock the car" is a subordinate clause, and cannot stand alone as a sentence. Indeed, this clause is essential to the preceding sentence, because it indicates what Denise remembered.

3. B: The alternative version is too wordy. It is unnecessary to say were involved in bringing when the same meaning can be conveyed by brought. In writing, it is best to use the minimum number of words necessary.

4. B: In the other version, it is not totally clear what they and them refer to in the second clause. The reader may not be able to tell whether the officers or the civilians should be talking more.

5. B: In the other version of the sentence, the subject of the introductory clause is unclear. It is not apparent whether Dave or his teacher was seventeen. Of course, the reader probably will guess that the writer meant to say that Dave was seventeen, but this guesswork should not be required of a reader. The correct version of the sentence makes it plain that the event in question occurred when Dave was seventeen.

6. A: The other version would be considered a run-on sentence, because there is no conjunction (like and or but) after the comma. The correct version of the sentence uses a colon, a mark of punctuation that can function in much the same way as a conjunction. In this case, it introduces the answer to the question posed by the first part of the sentence.

7. A: In the other version of the sentence, the subject is singular but the subsequent pronouns are plural. It is common for them to be used this way, but it is ungrammatical and potentially confusing for the reader. In the correct version of the sentence, the subject has been made plural to agree with the pronouns.

8. B: The other version is grammatically correct but awkward. Rephrasing the sentence to eliminate the introductory clause makes it much easier to read.

9. A: The other version is a run-on sentence, in which two independent clauses are not connected properly. Because the second clause clarifies the first, it is appropriate to separate them with a semicolon.

10. B: When a sentence contains a list (in this case, a list of the things a police officer does a great deal of), the items in the list should be expressed in the same grammatical terms. Because "lifting weights" includes a verb, every other item in the list should include a verb as well. In the incorrect version of the sentence, it sounds as if a police officer must lift paperwork and weights. There are other correct ways that this sentence could be written, for instance, "Being a police officer involves a great deal of weights and paperwork." In this version, none of the items in the list are accompanied by a verb. The important thing is for the treatment of list items to be consistent. In grammar, this is known as parallel structure.

11. A: The incorrect sentence has two different subjects: "one" in the first clause and "you" in the second. Although the reader would probably be able to make sense of this sentence, it is unnecessarily confusing. In the correct version of the sentence, there is a single subject.

12. A: Commas are necessary to set off the two subordinate clauses, "which was set at the back of the property" and "including a shed." The sentence becomes much easier to read when the commas are added, because the reader is encouraged to take the appropriate pauses.

13. B: In the other version of the sentence, the initial clause does not indicate who read the manual. The reader will probably guess that Linda was the reader, but it is also possible that there was some other, unnamed manual reader. The incorrect version of the sentence is needlessly confusing.

14. A: The other version of the sentence is redundant. There is no need to say both "was employed" and "worked." The correct version of the sentence eliminates one of these phrases and makes the sentence easier to read. It would also be correct to write, "Dr. Gerard was employed at the precinct station as a staff psychologist."

15. B: The other version of the sentence has a confusing introductory clause. The wording of that version creates the impression that the smell of almonds, rather than Kevin, was entering the house.

Spelling

16. B: absence

17. B: twelfth

18. D: cemetery

19. D: vicious

20. B: rhythm

21. B: miscellaneous

22. A: conscious

23. C: miniature

24. C: receipt

25. A: seize

26. B: precede

27. C: burglar

28. A: weird

29. A: sergeant

30. B: accommodations

Vocabulary

31. C: Persistent most nearly has the same meaning as tenacious. Both of them refer to the quality of never giving up, or continuing to attempt something no matter the resistance or the result.

32. B: Believable most nearly has the same meaning as credible. Both of these words mean easy to agree with or believe.

33. D: Supporter most nearly has the same meaning as partisan. Both of these words refer to people who endorse and contribute to the success of a particular cause.

34. A: Argument most nearly has the same meaning as premise. Both of them refer to an idea or concept that is being advanced.

35. B: Compliment most nearly has the same meaning as accolade. Both of them are nouns that mean praise or positive words.

36. C: Continuous most nearly has the same meaning as perpetual. Both of these adjectives refer to things that never stop or are ongoing.

37. A: Invalidate most nearly has the same meaning as rescind. Both of these verbs mean to declare something null and void.

38. D: Produce most nearly has the same meaning as generate. These verbs mean to make or create.

39. B: Conflicting most nearly has the same meaning as incompatible. Both of these adjectives refer to people or things that disagree, do not get along, or do not go well together.

40. C: Wealth most nearly has the same meaning as prosperity. Both of them refer to affluence or an abundance of riches.

41. C: Newcomer most nearly has the same meaning as novice. Both refer to a person who is new or is just beginning to learn something.

42. B: Frankness most nearly has the same meaning as candor. Both of these nouns mean total honesty, even when what is being expressed is unpopular or unpleasant.

43. D: Cautious most nearly has the same meaning as prudent. Both of these words mean careful and safe.

44. A: Inherent most nearly has the same meaning as innate. Both of these adjectives mean built-in or ingrained.

45. B: Passive most nearly has the same meaning as submissive. These words refer to people that are not in charge and do not attempt to be in control.

Reading Comprehension

46. C: Based on the passage, the most accurate statement is that Randy Barron could not navigate his wheelchair down a steep ramp. Indeed, the second sentence of the passage states that "the ramp going down to the Recorder of Deeds office was too steep for him to safely use his wheelchair." The passage does not indicate that the door to the county building was locked or too narrow, though it does state that there was not enough room for Barron to maneuver his wheelchair. The passage does not say anything about Barron having a hard time going up a ramp: the only ramp mentioned in the passage is one that Barron must go down.

47. A: Based on the passage, the most accurate statement is that Randy Barron's acquisition of a marriage license was made more difficult by barriers to accessibility. This is the main idea of the passage, which begins by describing Barron's excitement and then discusses the various problems that made his task harder. The final sentence summarizes the idea: "Barriers to accessibility mean that people...will not be able to fully benefit from services and programs." The passage never states that Barron was unable to get married at all, just that the process was more difficult than necessary. The passage never states that the door was locked or that Washington County forbids handicapped people from getting married. Finally, there is no suggestion that the Recorder of Deeds should switch offices with another county employee. This switch would do nothing to diminish the problems of the handicapped.

48. D: Based on the passage, the most accurate statement is that there are special concerns for a 911 dispatcher when dealing with the mentally ill. This statement is not made explicitly, but it is the main idea of the passage nonetheless. The passage indicates in several ways that 911 call takers should receive special training for dealing with cases involving the mentally ill. The passage does not state that a 911 dispatcher is not allowed to inquire about a person's history of mental illness: on the contrary, the first sentence states that this is one of the first inquiries the call taker should make. The passage describes the special concerns and protocol for dealing with the mentally ill, so clearly it does not state that the mentally ill should receive the same treatment as everyone else. Finally, the passage states that a list of questions should be developed by "members of the coordinating group with mental health backgrounds," not call takers.

49. B: Based on the passage, the most accurate statement is that it is important for 911 dispatchers to collect information quickly. The passages specifically states that "all call takers should receive training on how to collect the most useful information quickly." The passage does not indicate that 911 operators get more than one chance to acquire key information: on the contrary, the passage suggests that vital information must be collected as quickly as possible. The passage mentions that the call taker should inquire about the mentally ill person's access to weapons, but it does not provide any information about the amount of access given to the mentally ill relative to other citizens. Finally, the passage directly states that all 911 operators should be trained in obtaining the key information about the mentally ill.

50. B: Based on the passage, the most accurate statement is that the use of less-lethal technologies reduces the danger for officers. The third sentence of the passage states that other options "potentially are more dangerous to officers and suspects." It could be presumed that the use of more aggressive weapons leads to more instances of violent retaliation by suspects, as well as more instances in which the officer's own weaponry is turned against him or her. As for the other answer choices, the passage states directly that "almost all larger law enforcement agencies have written policies about the use of less-lethal force." Also, the passage does not indicate that officers are typically required to use the maximum amount of force whenever possible; instead, it states that officers are taught to use the higher levels of force only in the most severe circumstances. Finally, stun grenades are mentioned as an example of a less-lethal technology.

51. D: Based on the passage, the most accurate statement is that less-lethal technology is an alternative to rather than a replacement for traditional physical force methods. The passage makes clear that less-lethal technology will not be suitable in all situations, and that there may be some cases in which higher levels of force are required. The assessment of danger is not entirely left to the judgment of the officer. According to the passage, "many agencies…have training programs to help evaluate dangerous circumstances." At another point, the passage describes how many large agencies have an "approved use-of-force continuum" that helps officers determine the appropriate response. Finally, the passage gives Tasers, not stun grenades, as an example of a conducted-energy device.

52. A: Using the above coding system, the call number A-3-8 would identify day; traffic division, bicycle; north side.

53. C: Using the above coding system, the call number C-4-33 would identify graveyard; patrol division, platoon 1; downtown.

54. B: Based on the passage, the most accurate statement is that emergency vehicle sirens help improve their visibility. Though this may seem counterintuitive, sirens and horns improve visibility simply by encouraging other drivers to look in the direction of the vehicle. As the passage states, these features are "designed to draw attention…even when drivers are not actively looking." The passage does not say that it is more important for an emergency vehicle to be visible when it is in motion: it implies that visibility is important both when the vehicle is in motion and when it is stopped. Next, the passage does not state that weather and time of day are the *only* environmental conditions that affect a vehicle's visibility, though these are given as examples of important environmental conditions. Furthermore, the passage never suggests that emergency vehicles are always painted in special colors to improve their visibility, though the information provided by the passage does suggest that this would be a good idea.

55. A: Based on the passage, the most accurate statement is that emergency responders must be visible when in motion and when stopped. This is made clear in the first paragraph, when the passage describes how an emergency vehicle must be seen "as it navigates through traffic" and "on the side of the road." It is not true that only emergency vehicles have features that provide information to other drivers: for one thing, all cars have

warning lights that tell other cars when they are braking. The passage does not state that retro-reflective lighting is useless during the day. Finally, the passage states that other drivers need to know several factors about an emergency vehicle, including its "size, position, speed, and direction of travel" in order to respond correctly.

56. D: Based on the passage, the most accurate statement is that in Buffalo, parking meter mechanics do not have access to the coin canisters. This fact is made plain in the first sentence, where it states that James Bagarozzo (and other parking meter mechanics) "didn't have access to [the] coin canisters and was not authorized to collect money." With this in mind, it is clear that James Bagarozzo was not responsible for collecting the money from parking meters in Buffalo. Similarly, there is no indication that Bagarozzo had a criminal history before he began working as a parking meter mechanic. Finally, the passage does not suggest that Bagarozzo deposited the money into his bank account: on the contrary, it states that he took it to the bank and exchanged it for cash.

57. A: Based on the passage, the most accurate statement is that most police departments do not use body-worn cameras. The first sentence states that a recent survey found that around three-quarters of police departments do not use body-worn cameras. The passage describes the pros and cons of using these cameras, so it is inaccurate to state that there are no disadvantages to their use. Among the disadvantages is the cost of the cameras, which are not inexpensive and which require costly accessories and training. Finally, body-worn cameras do not make police officers transparent; rather, they encourage departmental transparency insofar as they make it difficult for police officers to misrepresent their actions.

58. A: Based on the passage, the most accurate statement is that body-worn cameras are not right for every police department. The last sentence of the passage states that there is as yet not enough research for law enforcement executives to properly decide whether to obtain these cameras. This suggests that the costs may be too high for some departments. From this last sentence, it is clear that there is not a large body of research on this technology. The passage does not indicate whether police officers prefer to wear the cameras. Lastly, the passage does not state that the cameras are difficult to use, though it does mention that training is required.

59. B: Based on the passage, the most accurate statement is that arson investigators do not always find evidence of criminal activity at a fire scene. The last sentence states that investigators "*may* find evidence…which *may* indicate criminal activity." In other words, investigators do not always find such evidence. Similarly, the passage indicates that some burn patterns suggest criminal activity, but not that all do. The passage does not state that arson investigators question suspects and try to establish motive. Moreover, the passage does not indicate that the investigators themselves analyze the evidence, simply that the evidence is analyzed.

60. B: Based on the passage, the most accurate statement is that high-speed pursuits require officers to make the right decision in an instant. The passage states this in the last sentence. There is no indication that high-speed pursuits cause more injuries than deaths.

The passage states that most high-speed pursuits last fewer than six minutes. Finally, the passage does not assert that high-speed pursuits are the largest cause of officer fatalities, though it does indicate that these pursuits are hazardous to officers.

61. B: Based on the passage, the most accurate statement is that CEDs are not totally safe, but they are safer than conventional methods of force. This fact is made plain in the last sentence, where the author states that conducted-energy devices can reduce injuries to both officers and suspects relative to conventional methods of force.

62. A: Based on the passage, the most accurate statement is that crimes are not classified while victims are being interviewed. On the contrary, the passage states directly that "during data processing, a computer program classifies each event into one type of crime, based on the entries on a number of items on the survey questionnaire." The protocol, then, is for police to help victims fill out a survey, the results of which are used by a computer to classify the crime. The passage makes plain in the first sentence that "law enforcement are required to follow this protocol at all times," so it would be incorrect to say that it only needs to be observed occasionally. Crime classification is not based on the first offense reported by the victim, but rather on "the most serious event that occurred." Finally, the passage does not suggest that police officers have control over the items on the survey questionnaire. Though the passage does not state this directly, it implies that the survey questionnaire consists of a standard set of questions so that classification will be performed in a consistent manner.

63. C: Based on the passage, the most accurate statement is that sexual assault is a more serious crime than motor vehicle theft. This judgment is made according to the hierarchy given in the final sentence. According to this hierarchy, the most serious event is rape and the least serious event is theft.

64. A: Based on the passage, the most accurate statement is that strong relationships between owners and employees decrease the incidence of employee theft. This is indicated at several points in the passage, such as when the writer states that employers should "get to know [their] employees." The passage does not suggest that thriving businesses are less likely to have employee theft. Likewise, the passage does not state that employees should lead crime prevention practices, merely that they should be involved. Finally, the passage does not state that competition between employees will reduce employee theft, though it does argue that offering competitive salary rates will discourage theft.

65. A: Based on the passage, the most accurate statement is that sometimes employees steal because they feel that they are underpaid. The second sentence of the passage states that "employees who are treated fairly and generously are less likely to steal," and the last sentence encourages employers to "make sure your salary rates are competitive." Clearly, well-compensated employees will be less inclined to steal from their employers. There is no suggestion, however, that employees should be paid as much as their employers, or that employee theft is the most common crime in the workplace. Finally, though the passage does imply that profit-sharing programs can be a useful strategy for reducing employee theft, there is no assertion that these programs always are successful in doing so.

Cloze

66. took

67. was

68. into

69. from

70. been

71. when

72. an

73. been

74. at

75. this

76. open

77. were

78. prints

79. was

80. shoes

81. after

82. there

83. or

84. from

85. and

86. police

87. thief

88. not

89. with

90. could

91. knew

92. also

93. help

94. were

95. list

96. in

97. store

98. by

99. that

100. with

101. card

102. search

103. was

104. he

105. to

Reasoning

106. D: The next number in the series is 30. In this series, each successive number is three less than the number that preceded it. So, to find the next number in the series, simply subtract three from the last number given.

107. C: The correct order of finish is Bruce, Aaron, and then Carl. According to the prompt, Aaron finished after Bruce but before Carl. Bruce, therefore, must have finished before Carl as well. Since Aaron was in between the other two finishers, the order of finish must be Bruce, Aaron, and Carl.

108. A: The word *ramp* is not like the other three. A ramp, house, castle, or shack is a place where someone could live.

109. B: The pattern is a recurring series of three numbers: 12, 27, and 36. Therefore, a 27 would follow the 12.

110. D: There is not enough information to solve this problem. There is no indication as to where the two girls who tied finished in relation to Ellen and Gretchen. That is, Fiona and Helen may have finished ahead of Ellen and Gretchen, in between them, or after them. Therefore, it is impossible to say who finished in second place.

111. B: Philip scored a 78. Since Edgar scored ten points worse than Dave, who got a 92, then Edgar must have gotten an 82. If Philip scored four points worse, then he got a 78.

112. B: The next number in the series is 37. In this pattern, the gap between each successive pair of numbers is 1, then 3, then 5, etc. In other words, the gap increases by two each time. Therefore, since the difference between 17 and 26 is 9, the difference between the next two numbers will be 11, and so the next number in the sequence will be 37.

113. D: There is not enough information to answer this question. It is clear that both Frank and Henry weigh more than George, but it is impossible to tell which of those two weighs more.

114. B: The word container is not like the other three. *Fierce*, *quiet*, and *grainy* are all adjectives: that is, they are words used to describe things or ways of doing things. *Container*, on the other hand, is a noun. Nouns refer to people, places, or things.

115. C: The next number in the series is 15. In this pattern, the gaps between the decreasing numbers alternate between seven and one. Since the gap between 23 and 16 is seven, the next number will be one fewer than sixteen.

116. B: The word is not like the other three. Milk, juice, and soda are beverages, or things that a person drinks. A banana is a food.

117. C: The next number in the series is 22. The numbers in this series increase by one more with each successive term. So, there is a gap of 1 between the first two numbers, a gap of 2 between the second and third numbers, a gap of 3 between the third and fourth numbers, and so on.

118. B: Yolanda finished in last place. If Xavier finished ahead of Zeke, and Zeke finished ahead of Yolanda, then Xavier must have finished ahead of Yolanda as well. Therefore, Yolanda finished in last place.

119. C: The next number in the series is 37. This pattern is just two alternating numbers, 37 and 32. A 37 will always follow a 32.

120. A: The word *planet* is not like the other three. A remote control, a coat, and an elevator all have buttons, but a planet does not.

121. B: The next number in the series is 11. In this series, each pair of numbers is separated by a difference of six, but each successive pair is one more than the last. So, the next pair would be 11 and 17.

Practice Test #2

Clarity

Instructions: In the following pairs of sentences, identify the sentence that is most clearly written. If sentence "a" is more clear than sentence "b," mark "a" on your answer sheet. If sentence "b" is more clear than sentence "a," mark "b" on your answer sheet.

1.   a. When Frank arrived at the festival, he remembered that he had left his credit card at the store and must go back to retrieve it.
       b. When Frank arrived at the festival, he remembered that he had left his credit card at the store, so he had to go back to retrieve it.

2.   a. Victor, who had never been to Canada, was nonetheless accused of smuggling cigarettes over the border, which was a felony.
       b. Victor who had never been to Canada was nonetheless accused of smuggling cigarettes over the border which was a felony.

3.   a. In pursuit of the suspect, he dodged trash cans, boxes, and through red lights.
       b. In pursuit of the suspect, he dodged trash cans, leapt over boxes, and ran through red lights.

4.   a. He could not be held because the investigators had made several errors during the collection of evidence.
       b. The reason he could not be held was because the investigators had made several errors during the collection of evidence.

5.   a. The officer courteously asked the crowd of onlookers to stand back and avoid trampling the garden.
       b. The officer courteously asked the crowd of onlookers to stand back and to please avoid trampling the garden.

6.   a. To keep her daughter safe, the rat poison had to be locked away.
       b. To keep her daughter safe, Sheryl had to lock the rat poison away.

7.   a. We prepared for our guest a special dish consisting of rice, sausage, and spicy peppers.
       b. We prepared a special dish for our guest consisting of rice, sausage, and spicy peppers.

8.   a. For many asthma sufferers who also have allergies struggle during the spring.
       b. Many asthma sufferers who also have allergies struggle during the spring.

9.   a. Every candidate must complete the exercises in the training manual before class tomorrow.
        b. It is essential that every candidate must complete the exercises in the training manual before class tomorrow.

10.   a. To identify the correct punishment, listed in the appropriate section of the penal code.
        b. The correct punishment is listed in the appropriate section of the penal code.

11.   a. Lawmakers hoped to decrease the rate of domestic violence by raising the penalty for first-time offenders.
        b. Hoping to decrease the rate of domestic violence, the new law raised the penalty for first-time offenders.

12.   a. During the review of the investigation, the officers noticed some differences in the witness' stories were missed during the investigation.
        b. During their review, the officers noticed that some differences in the witness' stories had been missed in the initial investigation.

13.   a. Darnell would learn that the benefits of restraint were much greater than those of impulsiveness.
        b. Darnell would learn that the benefits of restraint were much greater than impulsiveness.

14.   a. The coroner, an essential position in the department, responsible for gathering forensic information from the deceased.
        b. The coroner is an essential employee in the department, since he or she is responsible for gathering forensic information from the deceased.

15.   a. Francine felt that her daughter would not be protected until they moved to a new city.
        b. Francine felt that her daughter's safety would not be protected until they moved to a new city.

Spelling

Instructions: In the following sentences, choose the correct spelling of the missing word. Mark on your answer sheet the letter that identifies the correct choice.

16. Even though the last few weeks had been hard, Barry knew he had much to be _____ about in his life.
    a. greatful
    b. grateful
    c. greatfull
    d. gratefull

17. He always read the newspaper to see _____ there were any good jobs in the classified advertising section.
    a. weather
    b. wether
    c. wather
    d. whether

18. To be _____ in any endeavor, one must commit oneself entirely.
    a. successful
    b. succesful
    c. successfull
    d. sucesful

19. The manager hoped he could _____ last month's numbers without requiring any help from the rest of the department.
    a. exeed
    b. exceed
    c. excede
    d. exsede

20. Hiking, gardening, and bridge were more than enough to fill up all of her _____ time.
    a. leesure
    b. lesure
    c. leisure
    d. liesur

21. Even though he was an adult by any measure, Kevin nevertheless listened carefully to the _____ of his parents.
    a. judgment
    b. judgement
    c. jugement
    d. judgemente

22. A leader should never _____ the importance of earning the support of his or her followers.
    a. undarrate
    b. undarate
    c. underate
    d. underrate

23. The diner was understaffed, but the managers were still willing to _____ a large party of tourists.
    a. acommodate
    b. accommodate
    c. acomodate
    d. accomodate

24. The witness _____ that she had seen the suspect enter the residence through a bedroom window.
    a. alledged
    b. alleged
    c. illeged
    d. aledged

25. If the _____ is correct, we will have enough fuel to make it back to Sacramento.
    a. gauge
    b. gage
    c. guage
    d. gaug

26. The car should run for at least another hundred thousand miles, so long as you get all the usual _____.
    a. maintenance
    b. maintanance
    c. meintenence
    d. mentainance

27. After several hours of deliberation, the jury decided to _____ the defendant on all charges.
    a. aquit
    b. acuit
    c. acquit
    d. aqcuit

28. "Your performance on the exam should _____ you," the teacher sternly remarked to Sally.
   a. embarrass
   b. ambaress
   c. embaress
   d. embarass

29. Using your service _____ for personal business is typically forbidden by employers.
   a. vehical
   b. vehicle
   c. vehickle
   d. vihical

30. This award is given _____ to the officer who demonstrated the most bravery over the course of the last year.
   a. anually
   b. annally
   c. annually
   d. annully

Vocabulary

Instructions: In each of the following sentences, choose the word or phrase that most nearly has the same meaning as the underlined word. Mark on your answer sheet the letter that identifies the correct choice.

31. He did not miss an opportunity to repudiate the charges that had been brought against him.
    a. confirm
    b. deny
    c. congratulate
    d. reform

32. Her inept handling of the case convinced her supervisors that she was not ready for a promotion.
    a. worthless
    b. valuable
    c. ferocious
    d. awkward

33. Dina received every possible plaudit from her bosses after her superlative conduct during the investigation.
    a. praise
    b. expertise
    c. focus
    d. contrast

34. After a five-year absence from the workplace, he discovered that some of his old methods were now obsolete.
    a. incorrect
    b. reckless
    c. special
    d. outdated

35. He had to gather all of his resolve to make the final ascent up the mountain.
    a. delegate
    b. decide
    c. stagnate
    d. consider

36. She knew that her work problems were <u>transient</u>, but still she couldn't stop focusing on them to the point of distraction.
    a. impermanent
    b. fixed
    c. ghostly
    d. sedate

37. Florence knew she must <u>hasten</u> if she wanted to catch the final train of the day.
    a. delay
    b. accelerate
    c. flagellate
    d. forget

38. The recovery of millions of <u>counterfeit</u> dollars was a huge breakthrough in the case.
    a. coordinated
    b. supreme
    c. fake
    d. inferior

39. The room was already filled with bold and bright colors, so Sheila selected a more <u>neutral</u> tone for the walls.
    a. impartial
    b. life-like
    c. belligerent
    d. social

40. Community service is sometimes <u>punitive</u>, but it can also be enriching and inspiring.
    a. disciplinary
    b. engaged
    c. trivial
    d. defamatory

41. He could barely concentrate on his work problems while his <u>domestic</u> life was in such disarray.
    a. nightly
    b. household
    c. buoyant
    d. tranquil

42. He begged the judge for a <u>reprieve</u>, but the evidence against him was too strong.
    a. mercy
    b. collect
    c. defend
    d. pay back

43. The work in front of her was <u>tedious</u>, but she was determined to get through it all before lunch.
    a. exaggerated
    b. speedy
    c. cantankerous
    d. boring

44. The strongest perfume was not enough to <u>nullify</u> the aroma of the skunk.
    a. negate
    b. annoy
    c. destroy
    d. accumulate

45. Being wealthy or famous does not <u>preclude</u> one from being the victim of fraud.
    a. extend
    b. prevent
    c. collect
    d. salivate

Reading Comprehension

Instructions: Officers must read and understand a wide range of materials. This test is designed to measure your ability to read and understand various types of written material. Read each paragraph or passage and choose the statement that best answers the question. All questions pertain only to the material in the passage that precedes them. Choose your answer solely on the basis of the material contained in the passage. Mark the letter that identifies your choice in the space on your answer sheet. Do not spend too much time on any one item.

Questions 46 and 47 are based on the following passage:

Protective vests for law enforcement officers include ballistic-resistant and stab-resistant body armor that provides coverage and protection primarily for the torso. Different kinds of armor protect officers against different kinds of threats. Ballistic-resistant body armor protects against bullet penetrations and the blunt trauma associated with bullet impacts. These vests include soft body armor that protects against handgun bullets and less flexible tactical armor composed of soft and hard components that protect against rifle bullets. Stab-resistant body armor protects against knives and spikes. Manufacturers also make combination armor that protects against both types of threats. When purchasing body armor, law enforcement agencies must consider the kinds of threats their officers will likely face and choose body armor with suitable properties to protect against those threats.

46. Based on the preceding passage, which of the following statements is most accurate?
    a. There are specialized types of body armor for different situations.
    b. Stab-resistant body armor is useless against bullets.
    c. Ballistic-resistant protective vests typically provide full-body coverage.
    d. Law enforcement departments should all purchase the same type of protective vest.

47. Based on the preceding passage, which of the following statements is most accurate?
    a. There are special forms of body armor for protecting the lower body.
    b. Police officers must wear body armor at all times.
    c. Body armor is effective in all situations.
    d. The body armor that protects against handgun bullets is more flexible than the armor that protects against rifle bullets.

Questions 48 and 49 are based on the information listed below:

Radio code is the coding system for identifying units both inside and outside the department. There are three components to every radio code. Each of these components must be included when officers are dispatched. In this coding system, units are identified with three characters: a number designating the severity, a letter designating the location, and a number identifying the type of event.

Severity
1: Emergency
2: Urgent
3: Non-urgent

Location
A: Northeast
B: North
C: Northwest
D: West
E: Southwest
F: South
G: Southeast
H: East

Event type
1: Traffic offense
2: Domestic dispute
3: Public disorder
4: Drug offense

48. Using the above coding system, the call number 3-C-4 would signify:
    a. a non-urgent drug offense in the northwestern part of the city.
    b. an emergency traffic offense in the western part of the city.
    c. a non-urgent domestic dispute in the southeastern part of the city.
    d. an urgent public disorder in the southern part of the city.

49. Using the above coding system, the call number 1-G-2 would signify:
    a. an urgent traffic offense in the southeastern part of the city.
    b. an emergency traffic offense in the eastern part of the city.
    c. a domestic dispute emergency in the southeastern part of the city.
    d. a non-urgent drug offense in the northern part of the city.

Questions 50 and 51 are based on the following passage:

Because concern for elder abuse as a criminal issue is a fairly recent development, there are gaps in our knowledge about the extent and causes of such abuse. The majority of research on elder mistreatment has focused on victims; the motivations of abusers and the relationship between abusers and victims have received little attention. This produces an incomplete picture of the dynamics fueling elder abuse. Also, the field of research has relied heavily on the caregiver stress model, which holds that elder abuse can be attributed to the stress associated with providing care and assistance to frail, highly dependent elderly people. However, this model does not fit all situations and types of elder abuse. The field lacks an adequate guiding theory to explain the range of causes behind elder abuse and promote systematic data collection.

50. Based on the preceding passage, which of the following statements is most accurate?
a. Research based on the caregiver stress model has generated sufficient amounts of data.
b. There is still a great deal of research to be done on elder abuse.
c. Most research on elder abuse has focused on the motivations of abusers.
d. The caregiver stress model fails to address the cause of elder abuse.

51. Based on the preceding passage, which of the following statements is most accurate?
a. Not all elder abuse is caused by the stress of caring for the elderly.
b. The caregiver stress model is the most recent explanation for elder abuse.
c. Most research on elder abuse has focused on the relationship between abusers and victims.
d. The caregiver stress model is never appropriate for describing elder abuse.

Questions 52 and 53 are based on the following passage:

When a loved one is sentenced to prison, the emotional turmoil is difficult for everyone to handle. Perhaps the heaviest burden is felt by those who are unintentional victims of crime - children of incarcerated parents. Nationally, 7.3 million children have at least one parent in jail or prison. Sadly, 70 percent of these kids are doomed to follow in the same footsteps as their parents by becoming imprisoned at some point in their lives. In fact, children of incarcerated parents are five times more likely than their peers to commit crimes. However, these at-risk children are largely ignored before they get in trouble.

52. Based on the preceding passage, which of the following statements is most accurate?
    a. The children of incarcerated parents are no more likely than other children to be imprisoned later in life.
    b. The children of incarcerated parents should not receive special treatment.
    c. Children with both parents in jail are even more likely than children with one parent in jail to be imprisoned later in life.
    d. More than half of the children of incarcerated parents will be imprisoned at some point during their lives.

53. Based on the preceding passage, which of the following statements is most accurate?
    a. The spouses of incarcerated people are not defined as unintentional victims of crime.
    b. The children of incarcerated parents receive no special treatment at present.
    c. The children of incarcerated parents are more likely than other children to commit crimes at some point in their lives.
    d. More than 7 million children of incarcerated parents will themselves end up in jail.

Question 54 is based on the following passage:

Specialized responses to people with mental illnesses are an outgrowth of community policing and as such should reflect a partnership between a law enforcement agency and other stakeholder groups and individuals. Partners for the lead law enforcement agency should include mental health service providers, people with mental illnesses and their family members and loved ones, and mental health advocates. Any stakeholder may initiate the planning for the specialized response, but to take root, the lead law enforcement agency must fully embrace the effort.

54. Based on the preceding passage, which of the following statements is most accurate?
    a. Most law enforcement agencies are able by themselves to create effective policies for responding to the mentally ill.
    b. Planning a department's response to the mentally ill requires cooperation from several parties.
    c. Only the law enforcement agency can initiate the planning for a specialized response.
    d. The law enforcement agency is the most important party in planning the specialized response to the mentally ill.

Question 55 is based on the following passage:

Routine activity theory suggests that crime occurs when a motivated offender, a suitable target, and the lack of capable guardian converge in the same place at the same time. Criminals choose or find their targets within the context of their routine activities, such as traveling to and from work, or other activities such as shopping, and tend not to go too far out of their way to commit crimes.

55. Based on the preceding passage, which of the following statements is most accurate?
   a. The routine activity theory suggests that criminals operate in or near the places they already frequent.
   b. The work of a ring of sophisticated jewel thieves could be explained by the routine activity theory of crime.
   c. Routine activity theory suggests that most crime is committed by relatives of the victim.
   d. The routine activity theory does not account for the problem of employee theft.

Questions 56 and 57 are based on the following passage:

Federal law prohibits the sale of firearms or ammunition to juveniles and people who have been convicted of felonies and some violent misdemeanors. Federally mandated background checks keep these people from buying firearms at licensed dealers. Prohibited buyers may turn to the largely unregulated secondary market: gun sales between private individuals. The secondary market is a major source of guns used in crimes.

Why do people buy guns illegally? While some may buy them with the intent of using them in a crime, reasons can vary. Boston's Operation Ceasefire, a successful gun violence intervention, found that youths frequently acquire guns because they're afraid of being a target of violence from others.

56. Based on the preceding passage, which of the following statements is most accurate?
   a. Juveniles are allowed to purchase ammunition in some states.
   b. The federal government should eliminate background checks to reduce the illegal sale of firearms.
   c. The federal government regulates the secondary gun market.
   d. Background checks prevent juveniles and convicted criminals from purchasing guns at licensed stores.

57. Based on the preceding passage, which of the following statements is most accurate?
   a. People illegally purchase guns for many reasons.
   b. Guns purchased from licensed dealers are a part of the secondary market.
   c. Gun sales between private individuals are mostly used for criminal activity.
   d. Most of the people who purchase guns illegally do so for protection.

Questions 58 and 59 are based on the following passage:

You could call this scam a license to steal, and it certainly was – until it all came crashing down on the corrupt state employees and their accomplices who were selling California driver's licenses for cash. For at least three years, though, between 2009 and 2012, the scammers had a nearly seamless operation that netted a tidy profit. Here's how it worked: A man who owned a driving school let his students know that—for a price—he could guarantee them a license, even if they had already failed the driving test. Often they didn't even have to take the test, thanks to the man's connections at the Department of Motor Vehicles (DMV) office in El Cajon, California. Those willing to pay anywhere from $500 to $2,500 to corrupt DMV employees could get a license with no questions asked.

58. Based on the preceding passage, which of the following statements is most accurate?
    a. Students received fake exam results for free.
    b. The owner of a California driving school and DMV employees conspired to falsify the results of exams.
    c. The scam began in 2008.
    d. This scam would only have been possible in California.

59. Based on the preceding passage, which of the following statements is most accurate?
    a. Driving schools should be administered by the state.
    b. The state of California issues licenses to steal.
    c. This scam made driving more dangerous in California.
    d. A California driver's license usually costs at least $500.

Questions 60 and 61 are based on the following passage:

Public efforts to restrict firepower among those most prone to violence generally focus only on guns, not ammunition. For example, firearms dealers run the names of would-be gun buyers through an instant background check system to verify whether the person is legally allowed to own a gun. But although the same restrictions technically apply, ammunition purchasers are not subject to the same background check. This means that people who shouldn't be able to buy ammunition might be doing just that.

Research on illegal gun markets in the streets of Chicago shows that criminals already have a more difficult time buying ammunition than buying guns. If retail sales of ammunition were more tightly controlled to keep ammunition from falling into the wrong hands, would this squeeze the illegal market even further, and, perhaps, reduce gun violence?

60. Based on the preceding passage, which of the following statements is most accurate?
    a. People who are not allowed to buy firearms may be allowed to purchase ammunition.
    b. The legal efforts to reduce gun violence have focused primarily on ammunition.
    c. A background check is required for the purchase of ammunition.
    d. Ammunition is easier to purchase than guns themselves.

61. Based on the preceding passage, which of the following statements is most accurate?
    a. One way to reduce gun violence may be to control ammunition sales more tightly.
    b. There has been a sharp decline in gun violence in Chicago.
    c. It can be difficult to find the right ammunition for automatic weapons.
    d. Gun violence is the most common crime in Chicago.

Questions 62 and 63 are based on the following passage:
There is good evidence that early interventions in childhood, such as home visits by nurses, preschool intellectual enrichment programs, and parent management training, are effective in preventing delinquency. For example, an evaluation of the Elmira (NY) Nurse-Family Partnership program found that at age 15, children of the higher-risk mothers who received home visits had significantly fewer arrests than controls. Another follow-up when the children were 19 showed that the daughters (but not the sons) of mothers who received home visits had significantly fewer arrests and convictions.

62. Based on the preceding passage, which of the following statements is most accurate?
    a. Juvenile delinquency is the fault of parents.
    b. Delinquency cannot be totally eradicated.
    c. Juvenile delinquency mostly affects urban communities.
    d. Efforts to prevent juvenile delinquency should begin when children are very young.

63. Based on the preceding passage, which of the following statements is most accurate?
    a. Boys are more likely to be juvenile delinquents than girls.
    b. Parent management training should be mandatory.
    c. Elmira has the highest rate of juvenile delinquency in New York.
    d. The sons of mothers who had home visits did not have significantly fewer arrests and convictions at age 19.

Question 64 is based on the following passage:
Training must be provided to improve officers' responses to people with mental illnesses. Agencies may differ in the amount of training they offer: some will provide comprehensive training to all officers, some will provide this training only to a subset, and some will provide basic training to everyone in combination with more comprehensive training to a subset. At a minimum, a group of officers sufficient to cover all time shifts and geographic districts should receive extensive skills and knowledge training that builds on the more cursory information routinely given on this topic at recruit and in-service trainings. The chief law enforcement executive should ensure that training is also provided to supervisory and support personnel, such as midlevel managers, field training officers, call takers, and dispatchers, who advance the specialized program's operations.

64. Based on the preceding passage, which of the following statements is most accurate?
   a. Training for dealing with the mentally ill may be restricted to the officers who serve a particular geographic district.
   b. There is a standard training protocol for dealing with the mentally ill.
   c. Officers need special training to serve the mentally ill.
   d. In-service training never includes advice for dealing with the mentally ill.

Question 65 is based on the following passage:

A police force with integrity is one with little or no misconduct or corruption. In the past, most studies viewed the problem of misconduct as one of individual problem officers, the so-called bad apples on the force. More recent studies show that whites generally see misconduct as episodic and confined to individual officers, while blacks tend to see misconduct as a more entrenched aspect of policing.

65. Based on the preceding passage, which of the following statements is most accurate?
   a. A police force may have strong integrity and yet be filled with corruption.
   b. A white person would be more apt to see officer misconduct as inherent to the law enforcement system.
   c. Black people are more likely to be the victims of officer misconduct.
   d. Whites and blacks tend to view police misconduct differently.

Cloze

(66) _ _ _ _ began as a routine traffic stop turned into a thirty-minute, high-speed chase for Officer Terry Johnson. Officer Johnson was patrolling (67) _ _ _ stretch of highway just east of Waterboro when he observed a car traveling slightly faster than the (68) _ _ _ _ _ limit, which in that area was fifty-five miles per (69) _ _ _ _. As the car passed by, Officer (70) _ _ _ _ _ _ _ noticed that the car had a broken left taillight.

Officer Johnson turned (71) _ _ his siren, and pulled onto the highway behind the vehicle. At (72) _ _ _ _ _, it appeared that the driver would comply: the car pulled off the (73) _ _ _ _ onto the gravel shoulder and came to a (74) _ _ _ _. Officer Johnson noted the license plate number, gathered his equipment, (75) _ _ _ exited his service vehicle. Once he was approximately ten feet (76) _ _ _ _ from the car, however, the driver suddenly restarted his vehicle and drove away (77) _ _ great speed. Officer Johnson attempted to shoot out the back tire of the vehicle, (78) _ _ _ his shots bounced off the gravel to either side.

Flustered, Officer Johnson ran back to his service vehicle and immediately called for back-up. Then, he shifted the (79) _ _ _ into drive and sped off in pursuit. The fleeing vehicle (80) _ _ _ about a quarter mile ahead of him when he began, but he quickly made (81) _ _ the distance, with his siren blaring and lights flashing. The suspect vehicle, however, did not stop (82) _ _ _ _ he drew near behind it. Instead, it took a quick turn (83) _ _ _ the highway and on to a side street.

At this point, Officer Johnson had a decision (84) _ _ make. (85)_ _ _ _ _ _ he continue with his pursuit, and risk endangering other drivers and pedestrians by driving at high speed through a congested area, or should he rely on his back-up and the surveillance abilities (86) _ _ the department? He decided to continue with his pursuit for the present, at (87) _ _ _ _ _ until his colleagues could get organized and join the chase. Already, he (88) _ _ _ _ _ hear on the radio that a helicopter had taken off at department headquarters and was approaching the neighborhood of the chase. Officer Johnson knew (89) _ _ _ _ the chopper would be able to find the suspect more quickly if he stayed close, because the pilot could use the signal from the patrol car (90) _ _ _ guidance.

As all this was going on, the suspect and Officer Johnson continued to weave (91) _ _ _ _ _ _ _ traffic. There were a couple of close (92) _ _ _ _ _: at one point, the suspect drove up on the sidewalk slightly, and a couple of middle-aged pedestrians had to jump up onto the stoop of a house in order to avoid (93) _ _ _ _ _ hit. Officer Johnson focused (94) _ _ _ concentration on maintaining visual contact with the car, and with driving as safely (95) _ _ possible. He hoped (96) _ _ _ _ his fellow officers would be able to end the chase, which had already gone on for more than twenty (97) _ _ _ _ _ _ _.

Finally, (98) _ _ he rounded a narrow turn, Officer Johnson saw a roadblock ahead. (99) _ _ _ heart leapt with joy. (100) _ _ avoid a fatal accident, the suspect had no choice but to (101) _ _ _ _. Guns drawn, several officers raced to apprehend the driver, who exited the car with his (102) _ _ _ _ _ raised, resigned to his fate. An inspection of the (103) _ _ _ revealed several automatic weapons and a duffel bag full of illegal narcotics. Officer Johnson later received a commendation (104) _ _ _ _ the department for his performance (105) _ _ _ _ _ _ the chase.

Reasoning

Instructions: Officers often face situations in which they need to determine how different pieces of information relate to one another. In this section, you will be presented with information such as a group or ordered series of facts, numbers, letters, or words. Your task is to study the various pieces of information and try to understand how they relate to one another. Mark the letter that identifies your choice on your answer sheet.

106. Three of the following words are similar, while one is different. Select the one that is different.
 a. glad
 b. well
 c. happily
 d. quickly

107. Identify the next number in the series: 3, 5, 8, 10, 13, 15,
 a. 17
 b. 18
 c. 19
 d. 20

108. Denise is three months older than Ellen, who is two months younger than Francesca. Gertrude is four months older than Francesca. Who is the oldest?
 a. Denise
 b. Francesca
 c. Gertrude
 d. Ellen

109. Identify the next number in the series: 4, 6, 8, 4, 6, 8...
 a. 4
 b. 6
 c. 8
 d. 10

110. Sally, Fred, and Mary are siblings. Fred is ten years older than Mary, and Sally is twice as old as Mary. How old is Mary?
 a. 12
 b. 16
 c. 22
 d. Not enough information

111. Three of the following words are similar, while one is different. Select the one that is different.
    a. Colombia
    b. Connecticut
    c. Delaware
    d. Wyoming

112. Identify the next number in the series: 772, 727, 277, 772...
    a. 277
    b. 727
    c. 772
    d. Not enough information

113. Doris, Erma, and Francine are in a pie-eating contest. Doris eats seven pies, and Francine eats four fewer. Erma eats three more pies than Francine. How many pies does Erma eat?
    a. 4
    b. 5
    c. 6
    d. Not enough information

114. On their last French test, Jamal got a higher score than Lindsay, Lindsay got a higher score than Soo Yin. Jamal's score was slightly higher than Bert's. Who got the second-highest score in the class?
    a. Lindsay
    b. Bert
    c. Soo Yin
    d. Not enough information

115. Three of the following things are similar, while one is different. Select the one that is different.
    a. apple
    b. carrot
    c. banana
    d. plum

116. Identify the next number in the series: 7, 7, 7, 17, 7, 27, 7...
    a. 7
    b. 17
    c. 27
    d. 37

117. Three of the following things are similar, while one is different. Select the one that is different.
    a. book
    b. magazine
    c. typewriter
    d. newspaper

118. Larry, Darrell, and Stuart went fishing. Larry caught seven fish, Darrell caught twice as many, and Stuart caught five fewer than Darrell. How many fish did Stuart catch?
    a. 9
    b. 10
    c. 11
    d. 12

119. Identify the next number in the series: 23, 26, 28, 29, 23, 26, 28...
    a. 23
    b. 26
    c. 28
    d. 29

120. Three of the following things are similar, while one is different. Select the one that is different.
    a. boat
    b. car
    c. bicycle
    d. wagon

121. Identify the next number in the series: 1, 4, 6, 9, 11, 14, 16...
    a. 18
    b. 19
    c. 20
    d. 21

Answers and Explanations #2

Clarity

1. B: The other version of the sentence has a confusing mixture of verb tenses. In particular, the auxiliary verb *must* is awkward, because it suggests that Frank remembered that he had to go back and retrieve the credit card. Of course, Frank would not have remembered this, but rather would have realized this was necessary after remembering that he had left his credit card. In the correct version of the sentence, the word *so* demonstrates that having to go back to the store was a consequence of remembering that the card had been left behind.

2. A: The other version omits the commas, which are necessary to ensure the sense of the sentence. Even without the commas, the sentence is comprehensible, but appropriate punctuation encourages the reader to make the appropriate pauses. By signaling the rhythm of the sentence, punctuation improves clarity.

3. B: The other version of the sentence does not maintain a consistent structure as it lists the things he did in pursuit of the suspect. The addition of the preposition *through* complicates the reader's progress through the sentence. In addition, "dodging" red lights does not totally make sense. In the clearer version, an appropriate verb has been paired with each obstacle, and the sentence is much smoother.

4. A: The other version is too wordy. Specifically, the phrase "The reason… was because" is unnecessary. In the correct version of the sentence, this awkward construction has been removed and the result is a much smoother sentence.

5. A: The other version is incorrect because it does not treat the items in the list consistently. This sentence ends with a list of the things the officer was asking the crowd to do. There are several correct ways that this list could be presented, but the items in the list must be presented in the same way. In the incorrect version of the sentence, the first item is "to stand back" and the second is "to please avoid." The insertion of *please* makes the sentence harder to read, and in any case is unnecessary because the officer's request has already been described as courteous.

6. B: In the other version, the awkward use of the introductory clause makes it sound as if the rat poison was trying to keep her daughter safe. Of course, this would not be the interpretation of most readers, but nevertheless the sentence fails to identify the subject of the introductory clause. In the correct version, the subject is clear.

7. A: In the incorrect version, it sounds as if the guest rather than the dish consisted of rice, sausage, and spicy peppers. By rearranging the clauses, the correct version makes the meaning clear.

8. B: In the other version, the word *for* at the beginning is unnecessary. In fact, the addition of this word turns the sentence into a fragment.

9. A: The other version of the sentence is too wordy. Specifically, the phrases "it is essential" and "must" are redundant. The correct version of the sentence eliminates "it is essential that," and there is no change to the sentence's meaning. The sentence could also be written, "It is essential that every candidate complete the exercises...," but this version is slightly less concise than the correct version in this question.

10. B: The other version is a fragment because it does not have a subject. A reader would probably be able to make sense of the incorrect version, but the absence of proper grammar would be distracting.

11. A: The other version is incorrect because it sounds as if the new law was hoping, when of course a law cannot hope.

12. B: The other version has two main problems. First, it repeats the word investigation, which is redundant and clumsy. This sort of repetition slows the reader down and may lead to confusion. The other problem with this sentence is that it omits the word *that*, which changes the emphasis: specifically, the sentence makes it is unclear whether the stories or the differences in the stories were missed. The correct version avoids these problems.

13. A: In the other version of the sentence, the terms of the comparison are unclear. It appears to be saying that the benefits of restraint are better than impulsiveness itself, rather than the *benefits* of impulsiveness. This makes some sense, but it seems more likely that the author is trying to compare the benefits of restraint with the benefits of impulsiveness. The correct version of the sentence makes this comparison more apparent.

14. B: The other version has a couple of problems. To begin with, it is a fragment because it does not have a main verb. To be grammatically correct, the sentence would have to state, "The coroner...*is* responsible." Another problem with this sentence is that the subordinate clause refers to the coroner as a position rather than as a person. There are cases where it would be appropriate to discuss the coroner as a position rather than a person, but in this case the focus is on the tasks performed by the coroner, and tasks are performed by a person, not a job role.

15. A: The other version refers to protecting her daughter's safety, which makes less sense than simply protecting her daughter.

Spelling

16. B: grateful

17. D: whether

18. A: successful

19. B: exceed

20. C: leisure

21. A: judgment

22. D: underrate

23. B: accommodate

24. B: alleged

25. A: gauge

26. A: maintenance

27. C: acquit

28. A: embarrass

29. B: vehicle

30. C: annually

Vocabulary

31. B: *Deny* most nearly has the same meaning as *repudiate*. Both of these verbs mean to reject or turn one's back on.

32. D: *Awkward* most nearly has the same meaning as *inept*. Both of these adjectives mean something like clumsy, improper, or lacking in skill.

33. A: *Praise* most nearly has the same meaning as *plaudit*. Both of them refer to positive feedback or comments.

34. D: *Outdated* most nearly has the same meaning as *obsolete*. These adjectives both mean that something is old-fashioned and, specifically, not able to be used anymore because of its age, and because subsequent advances have made it useless.

35. B: *Decide* most nearly has the same meaning as *resolve*. Both of these verbs mean to make a choice.

36. A: *Impermanent* most nearly has the same meaning as transient. Both of these words refer to things that are passing or that will not exist for very long.

37. B: *Accelerate* most nearly has the same meaning as hasten. Both of them mean to speed up or increase the rate.

38. C: *Fake* most nearly has the same meaning as *counterfeit*. Both of these words are used to describe things that have been falsified or forged.

39. A: *Impartial* most nearly has the same meaning as *neutral*. Both of them mean not taking a side.

40. A: *Disciplinary* most nearly has the same meaning as *punitive*. Both of these words indicate the negative consequences of misdeeds.

41. B: *Household* most nearly has the same meaning as *domestic*. Both of these words refer to things that are done in one's own area, as opposed to in a foreign or non-native area.

42. A: *Mercy* most nearly has the same meaning as *reprieve*. Both of them mean a release from punishment or trouble.

43. D: *Boring* most nearly has the same meaning as *tedious*. Both of them mean uninteresting.

44. A: *Negate* most nearly has the same meaning as *nullify*. Both of these words mean to erase or reduce to nothing.

45. B: *Prevent* most nearly has the same meaning as *preclude*. Both of these words mean to act ahead of time to keep something from happening.

Reading Comprehension

46. A: Based on the passage, the most accurate statement is that there are specialized types of body armor for different situations. The passage makes this plain in the second sentence: "Different kinds of armor protect officers against different kinds of threats." The specialization of protective vests does not necessarily mean that these vests will provide no protection against other attacks: for instance, the passage does not state that stab-resistant body armor will be useless against bullets, merely that there are more specialized types of armor for this purpose. The first sentence indicates that protective vests generally cover the torso, and not the entire body. Finally, the main idea of the passage is that law enforcement departments should not all purchase the same protective vests, but should select the appropriate vests based on the hazards their officers are likely to encounter.

47. D: Based on the passage, the most accurate statement is that the body armor that protects against handgun bullets is more flexible than the armor that protects against rifle bullets. The passage indicates as much when it states that the tactical armor designed to protect against rifle bullets is "less flexible." There probably are special forms of body armor for protecting the lower body, but the passage does not mention them. It also does not state that police officers must wear body armor at all times. Finally, the passage does not suggest that body armor is effective in all situations.

48. A: Using the above coding system, the call number 3-C-4 would signify a non-urgent drug offense in the northwestern part of the city.

49. C: Using the above coding system, the call number 1-G-2 would signify a domestic dispute emergency in the southeastern part of the city.

50. B: Based on the passage, the most accurate statement is that there is still a great deal of research to be done on elder abuse. This is the main point of the passage, and is expressed in the first sentence: "there are gaps in our knowledge about the extent and causes of such abuse. The passage states that the caregiver stress model has not produced enough data, though it does address the cause of elder abuse (namely, the stress associated with caring for the elderly). Finally, the second sentence of the passage states that most research thus far has focused on the victims rather than the motivations of abusers.

51. A: Based on the passage, the most accurate statement is that not all elder abuse is caused by the stress of caring for the elderly. The caregiver stress model focuses on this cause, but the passage is clear that this explanation is inadequate for every situation. The passage does not state that the caregiver stress model is the most recent explanation for elder abuse, just that it is currently the most popular. The passage states that "little attention" has been paid to the relationship between abusers and victims. Finally, while the passage is clear that the caregiver stress model is not enough to explain every aspect of elder abuse, there is no suggestion that it is never appropriate for describing elder abuse.

52. D: Based on the passage, the most accurate statement is that more than half of the children of incarcerated parents will be imprisoned at some point during their lives. The passage states that 70 percent of these children will be imprisoned at some point. It also states that these children are five times more likely than their peers to commit crimes, which suggests that they are also more likely to go to jail. The passage does not state explicitly that children of incarcerated parents should receive special treatment, though the facts presented certainly lead to this conclusion. Finally, there is no mention that children with both parents in jail are even more likely than children with one parent in jail to be imprisoned later in life.

53. C: Based on the passage, the most accurate statement is that the children of incarcerated parents are more likely than other children to commit crimes at some point in their lives. According to the passage, in fact, the children of incarcerated parents are five times more likely than their peers to commit crimes. The spouses of incarcerated people could probably be defined as the unintentional victims of crime, but this passage does not do so. Rather, it identifies the children of the incarcerated as such. The passage does not state that these at-risk children receive no special treatment, though it does say that they are "largely ignored." Finally, the passage does not state that more than 7 million children of incarcerated parents will be imprisoned at some point. The passage does state that there are 7.3 million children with at least one parent in jail, but of these only 70 percent (a little over 5 million) will end up in jail themselves.

54. B: Based on the passage, the most accurate statement is that planning a department's response to the mentally ill requires cooperation from several parties. The passage states that the specialized response protocol "should reflect a partnership between a law enforcement agency and other stakeholder groups and individuals." The passage is clear that law enforcement departments are not able to create these policies on their own, but that they are a collaboration with several parties. Moreover, the passage does not state that this planning must be initiated by the law enforcement department itself. Finally, there is no indication that the law enforcement agency is the most important party in planning the specialized response; on the contrary, the passage is clear that there are many stakeholders.

55. A: Based on the passage, the most accurate statement is that the routine activity theory suggests that criminals operate in or near the places they already frequent. This is evident in the second sentence: "Criminals choose or find their targets within the context of their routine activities." The routine activity theory probably would not be a very good explanation of the work of a ring of sophisticated jewel thieves, since these groups would necessarily be working in many different places, and not just those with which they were normally acquainted. The routine activity theory would, however, account for the problem of employee theft, since this is a crime committed by people who are very familiar with the work setting. This passage does not state that routine activity theory suggests that most crime is committed by relatives of the victim.

56. D: Based on the passage, the most accurate statement is that background checks prevent juveniles and convicted criminals from purchasing guns at licensed stores. Of course, these people often acquire guns from other sources. The passage states that juveniles are prevented from purchasing ammunition by federal law, which would apply in every state. There is no suggestion that background checks should be eliminated: while this would perhaps reduce illegal sales, it would only be because juveniles and felons would be able to obtain guns through the normal channels. Finally, the passage states explicitly that the secondary gun market is unregulated.

57. A: Based on the passage, the most accurate statement is that people illegally purchase guns for many reasons. This is expressed in the second sentence of the second paragraph. The guns purchased from licensed dealers are part of the primary market. The passage does not suggest that gun sales between private individuals are mostly used for criminal activity. Finally, the passage mentions that some illegal gun purchases are made for protection, but does not argue that this is the reason for most of these purchases.

58. B: Based on the passage, the most accurate statement is that the owner of a California driving school and DMV employees conspired to falsify the results of exams. This passage describes a scheme that required the participation of both the driving school operator and state employees. The article indicates that applicants paid at least $500 for a license, and that the scam began in 2009. There is no suggestion that this scam would only have been possible in California.

59. C: Based on the passage, the most accurate statement is that this scam made driving more dangerous in the state of California. The article states that the scam enabled drivers to obtain a license "even if they had already failed the driving test." There is no suggestion in the passage that driving schools should be administered by the state. The state of California does not literally issue licenses to steal. Finally, the California driver's license does not cost $500: this was the lower end of the range charged by the scammers for unearned licenses.

60. D: Based on the passage, the most accurate statement is that ammunition is easier to purchase than guns themselves. The first paragraph describes how would-be buyers of ammunition are not subjected to the same background check as if they were purchasing a gun. These people are actually forbidden from buying ammunition as well as firearms, but the current laws are ineffective at preventing ammunition sales. The first sentence of the passage states that public efforts thus far have focused primarily on guns, not ammunition.

61. A: Based on the passage, the most accurate statement is that one way to reduce gun violence may be to control ammunition sales more tightly. This suggestion is made in the final sentence of the passage. There is no indication in the passage that there has been a sharp decline in gun violence in Chicago, or that gun violence is the most common crime there. Neither is there any suggestion that it can be difficult to find the right ammunition for automatic weapons.

62. D: Based on the passage, the most accurate statement is that efforts to prevent juvenile delinquency should begin when children are very young. The first sentence indicates that these early interventions can be crucial in reducing later misbehavior. There is no suggestion that delinquency is the fault of parents, although the passage is clear that parents have a major role in preventing delinquency. Similarly, it seems unlikely that juvenile delinquency could be totally eradicated, but the passage does not address this question. Finally, the passage does not state that juvenile delinquency mostly affects urban communities.

63. D: Based on the passage, the most accurate statement is that the sons of mothers who had home visits did not have significantly fewer arrests and convictions at age 19. However, the passage does indicate that the daughters of these mothers did have fewer arrests and convictions. Still, the description of this research does not suggest that boys are more likely to be juvenile delinquents than girls. The passage does not argue that parent management training should be mandatory, though this might be inferred from the results of the research. Finally, the passage does not suggest that Elmira has the highest rate of juvenile delinquency in New York; it was simply the site of the research.

64. C: Based on the passage, the most accurate statement is that officers need special training to serve the mentally ill. The first sentence makes this statement, and the rest of the passage supports it. The passage does not state that training may be restricted to the officers who serve a particular geographic district; rather, it suggests that there should be trained officers for all times and places within the jurisdiction. The passage also suggests that there are different types and levels of training for officers in different positions. Finally, the passage directly states that basic information about dealing with the mentally ill is provided during recruit and in-service trainings.

65. D: Based on the passage, the most accurate statement is that whites and blacks tend to view police misconduct differently. The last sentence of the passage indicates that whites view officer misconduct as a problem with individual officers, while blacks view it as a natural part of an unjust system. Based on the first sentence, it seems that a police force could not have integrity and be corrupt at the same time. Blacks, not whites, are more apt to see officer misconduct as inherent to the law enforcement system. Finally, the passage does not indicate whether blacks or whites are more likely to be the victims of officer misconduct.

Cloze

66. What

67. the

68. speed

69. hour

70. Johnson

71. on

72. first

73. road

74. stop

75. and

76. away

77. at

78. but

79. car

80. was

81. up

82. when

83. off

84. to

85. should

86. of

87. least

88. could

89. that

90. for

91. through

92. calls

93. being

94. his

95. as

96. that

97. minutes

98. as

99. His

100. To

101. stop

102. hands

103. car

104. from

105. during

Reasoning

106. A: The word *glad* is not like the other three. *Well*, *happily*, and *quickly* are all adverbs, which means that are used to describe verbs. *Glad* is an adjective.

107. B: The next number in the series is 18. In this pattern, the numbers increase every time, but the rate of increase alternates between two and three.

108. C: Gertrude is the oldest. One way to solve a problem of this type is to assign an arbitrary age to the first person and then determine the rest of the ages relative to that one. So, if Gertrude is ten months old, then Ellen is seven months old, Francesca is nine months old, and Gertrude is thirteen months old. Therefore, Gertrude is the oldest.

109. A: The next number in the series is 4. This is a recurring pattern of three numbers: 4, 6, and 8. After 8, the pattern begins again with 4.

110. D: There is not enough information to solve this problem. The prompt provides information about the order of their ages, but since no specific ages are given, it is impossible to calculate Mary's age.

111. A: The word Colombia is not like the other three. Connecticut, Delaware, and Wyoming are all names of states, while Colombia is the name of a country.

112. B: The next number in the series is 727. In this series, each successive number has the digits shift forward one place, with the first digit becoming the last. Therefore, 772 would be followed by 727.

113. C: Erma ate six pies. If Doris ate seven pies, and Francine ate four fewer, then Francine ate three. IF Erma ate three more pies than Francine, then she ate six.

114. D: There is not enough information to answer this question. It is clear that Jamal got the highest score, and that Lindsay got a higher score than Soo Yin, but it cannot be determined whether Lindsay or Bert had a higher score.

115. B: A carrot is not like the other three because it is a vegetable. Apples, bananas, and plums are all fruits.

116. D: The next number in the series is 37. In this pattern, 7 is followed by first another seven, and then another number. This second number has a seven in the ones place, but is ten greater each time the pattern recurs.

117. C: A typewriter is not like a book, magazine, or newspaper, because the latter three are all things one would read, while a typewriter is something that one would use to write.

118. A: Stuart caught nine fish. If Darrell caught twice as many fish as Larry, and Larry caught seven, then Darrell must have caught fourteen. Stuart caught five fewer than Darrell, so he must have caught nine.

119. D: The next number in the series is 29. The pattern is repeating groups of four numbers: 23, 26, 28, and 29. So, after each 28 will come a 29.

120. A: A boat is not like the other three. Cars, bicycles, and wagons all have wheels, while a boat does not.

121. B: The next number in the series is 19. In this pattern, the difference between each successive increasing term is alternately three and two. So, since the difference between 14 and 16 is two, the next term will be three greater than 16.

Practice Test #3

Clarity

Instructions: In the following pairs of sentences, identify the sentence that is most clearly written. If sentence "a" is more clear than sentence "b," mark "a" on your answer sheet. If sentence "b" is more clear than sentence "a," mark "b" on your answer sheet.

1.   a. Social scientists continue to debate the connection between crime and violent imagery in video games and movies.
     b. Social scientists continue to debate the connection between crime plus violent imagery in video games and movies.

2.   a. There are a number of open desks for new recruits along the back wall of the room.
     b. Along the back wall of the room, there are a number of open desks for new recruits.

3.   a. The police commissioner claimed that the conflicting information made it impossible for her to decide.
     b. The police commissioner claimed that the conflicting information made it impossible for her to come to a decision.

4.   a. Even though both Sterling and Fred are in the choir, he has a much better voice.
     b. Though Sterling and Fred are both in the choir, Sterling has a much better voice.

5.   a. As the victim drove home on Denver Boulevard, she was forced to the side of the road by another car.
     b. The victim drove home, down Denver Boulevard, when she was forced to the side of the road by another car.

6.   a. The investigative work performed by Chandra was much better than any other detective.
     b. The investigative work performed by Chandra was much better than that of any other detective.

7.   a. A productive day not only will include hard work but also will include rest and relaxation.
     b. A productive day not only will include hard work and also will include rest and relaxation.

8.   a. Kevin spent most of his time reading magazines, playing video games, and taking naps.
        b. Kevin spent most of his time reading magazines, playing video games, and take naps.

9.   a. The group of women she met for coffee occasionally asked her about her haircut.
        b. The group of women she occasionally met for coffee asked her about her haircut.

10.   a. The actions you are suggesting would be in violation of the established rules.
        b. The actions you are suggesting would violate the established rules.

11.   a. Driving to the crime scene, the car began to emit thick, black smoke.
        b. The car began to emit thick, black smoke while he was driving to the crime scene.

12.   a. Frank had lived there all his life, yet he did not know the suspect.
        b. Even though Frank had lived there all his life, yet he did not know the suspect.

13.   a. One of the students feels that the rules that apply to the class are too strict.
        b. One of the students feel that the rules that apply to the class are too strict.

14.   a. Many of the calls came from citizens who the officers knew personally or worked near the police station.
        b. Many of the calls came from citizens who the officers knew personally or who worked near the police station.

15.   a. During John's first lesson, the teacher asked him if he had any experience or if he ever read about famous artists.
        b. During John's first lesson, the teacher asked him if he had any experience and did he ever read about famous artists.

Spelling

Instructions: In the following sentences, choose the correct spelling of the missing word. Mark on your answer sheet the letter that identifies the correct choice.

16. After it had a few weeks to heal, the scar on Stan's wrist was barely _____.
    a. nodicable
    b. notissable
    c. noticable
    ~ d. noticeable

17. A quick search of the trunk established that the driver was in _____ of a large amount of contraband.
    a. posesion
    b. possession
    c. possesion
    d. posession

18. Felicia spent most of her time in the _____ reading about history and science.
    a. library
    b. liberry
    c. librerry
    d. librery

19. He declared that he would not sleep _____ the mess was totally cleaned up.
    a. antill
    b. until
    c. untill
    d. antil

20. Before Nell could see the doctor, she had to fill out a brief _____ about her medical history.
    a. questionerre
    b. questionnaire
    c. questonairre
    d. questionarre

21. Denise asked the clerk if there were any books she would _____ for a week at the beach.
    a. recommend
    b. reccomend
    c. recommennd
    d. recomend

22. He was very familiar with the risks of opening a new _____.
    a. resterant
    b. resturant
    c. restaurant
    d. restarrant

23. Daily _____ is one of the cornerstones of a healthy lifestyle and a generally positive mood.
    a. exsercise
    b. excercise
    c. exercise
    d. exorcise

24. There was plenty that Quincy wanted to say, but instead he held his _____.
    a. tongue
    b. tung
    c. tonge
    d. tungue

25. The food was good, but the tiny portions could not help but _____ the starving customers.
    a. disappoint
    b. dissapoint
    c. disapoint
    d. dessapoint

26. It was determined that the rock slide was only _____ related to the recent blizzard.
    a. incedentally
    b. incidentally
    c. incidently
    d. incidenatally

27. After tearing failed to work, Owen finally had to use _____ to remove the tag from his new sweater.
    a. sizzers
    b. sissors
    c. scissors
    d. scisors

28. For Lonnie, even getting bailed out by his ex-wife was _____ to another night in the county jail.
    a. prefarable
    b. preferable
    c. prefferable
    d. preferrable

29. Because he had never lived in a city, his _____ parking skills were undeveloped.
    a. parallel
    b. paralel
    c. parulell
    d. perralel

30. After a _____ review of the case files, the detective decided that several of the initial leads had been handled poorly.
    a. through
    b. thorough
    c. thorow
    d. thurrow

Vocabulary

Instructions: In each of the following sentences, choose the word or phrase that most nearly has the same meaning as the underlined word. Mark on your answer sheet the letter that identifies the correct choice.

31. A <u>coherent</u> story would have helped his chances better than the stream of nonsense he provided.
    a. plausible
    b. frantic
    c. convincing
    d. understandable

32. In an organization with poor morale, employees may try to <u>subvert</u> the goals of their managers.
    a. support
    b. undermine
    c. freshen
    d. embolden

33. Viola felt there was no way to get the information she needed and not <u>protract</u> the conversation further.
    a. deliver
    b. enfold
    c. extend
    d. contend

34. Prunella did not see the cookies get taken, but she believed she could identify the <u>culprit</u>.
    a. fool
    b. humanitarian
    c. perpetrator
    d. breakfast

35. Darrel was allowed to remain on the scene so long as he did not <u>interfere</u> with the investigation.
    a. meddle
    b. confer
    c. delegate
    d. fend off

36. Despite the <u>abundant</u> trout in the river, Lorenzo and his son went all afternoon without even a bite.
    a. extreme
    b. plentiful
    c. improper
    d. collected

37. Instead of issuing a jail sentence, the judge elected to <u>levy</u> a strong fine against the offender.
    a. deny
    b. flag
    c. tariff
    d. impose

38. He hoped that his long apology would <u>appease</u> the disgruntled shopkeeper.
    a. anger
    b. satisfy
    c. conquer
    d. model

39. Loretta's <u>amiable</u> personality kept her from getting into too much trouble with her parents.
    a. possessive
    b. qualified
    c. friendly
    d. pugnacious

40. The size of the offer almost persuaded him to <u>forsake</u> the family business and move to the big city.
    a. betray
    b. ignore
    c. impersonate
    d. contain

41. He has a warm heart, and can express <u>empathy</u> for even the most immoral offenders.
    a. criticism
    b. compassion
    c. collaboration
    d. extension

42. At first he was worried, because he knew they could never <u>duplicate</u> their amazing performance in the first match.
    a. fragment
    b. replicate
    c. detach
    d. demonstrate

43. Aaron tried to be <u>punctual</u>, but he always underestimated how long it would take him to get across town.
   a. timely
   b. slight
   c. delayed
   d. minor

44. Brenda felt a great deal of <u>animosity</u> towards her coworkers after they blamed her for the mishap.
   a. concern
   b. cooperation
   c. hatred
   d. contentment

45. He wrote down a list of facts he could use to <u>rebut</u> the arguments made against him.
   a. confirm
   b. disprove
   c. detail
   d. anticipate

Reading Comprehension

Instructions: Officers must read and understand a wide range of materials. This test is designed to measure your ability to read and understand various types of written material. Read each paragraph or passage and choose the statement that best answers the question. All questions pertain only to the material in the passage that precedes them. Choose your answer solely on the basis of the material contained in the passage. Mark the letter that identifies your choice in the space on your answer sheet. Do not spend too much time on any one item.

Questions 46 and 47 are based on the following passage:

Crime does not occur evenly over the landscape. It is clustered in small areas, or hot spots, that account for a disproportionate amount of crime and disorder. For example, in Minneapolis, 3 percent of the city's addresses accounted for 50 percent of calls for service to the police in one study. In Jersey City, NJ, about 4 percent of streets and intersection areas generated nearly half of the city's narcotics arrests and almost 42 percent of the disorder arrests. In addition to location, crime and public disorder tend to concentrate at certain times of the day or week. Assaults, for example, occur most frequently between 3:00 a.m. and 7:00 a.m. when streets are largely vacant. Residential burglaries mostly occur during daytime hours when residents are not home. Incidents of driving under the influence occur more frequently in areas with a large number of bars or liquor stores.

46. Based on the preceding passage, which of the following statements is most accurate?
   a. Crime tends to occur more often in particular areas.
   b. Incidents of driving under the influence are more common along main roads.
   c. Minneapolis police have ignored much of the city.
   d. Residential burglaries usually occur during the night.

47. Based on the preceding passage, which of the following statements is most accurate?
   a. Police should open stations in hot spots.
   b. Public disorder usually occurs between three and seven in the morning.
   c. Assaults are more likely to occur in populated areas.
   d. Some times and places require more attention from police.

Questions 48 and 49 are based on the information listed below:

Radio code is the coding system for identifying units both inside and outside the department. There are three components to every radio code. Each of these components must be included when officers are dispatched. In this coding system, units are identified with three characters: a letter designating the event, a number designating the level of emergency, and a number identifying the area.

Event
A: Domestic dispute
B: Burglary
C: Drug offense
D: Assault
E: Harassment
F: Public intoxication
G: Traffic violation
H: Disorderly conduct

Level of emergency
1: Emergency
2: Urgent
3: Non-urgent

Area
1: Shackleford Banks
2: Financial District
3: Sloan Street
4: Little Italy
5: Government Plaza
6: Morningside Heights
7: Ashford Terrace

48. Using the above coding system, the call number F-2-1 would signify:
    a. an urgent public intoxication incident at Shackleford Banks.
    b. an assault emergency on Sloan Street.
    c. a non-urgent traffic violation on Morningside Heights.
    d. a non-urgent traffic violation in the Financial District.

49. Using the above coding system, the call number B-2-5 would signify:
    a. an urgent burglary incident at Government Plaza.
    b. a public intoxication emergency on Sloan Street.
    c. an urgent disorderly conduct incident in Little Italy.
    d. a harassment emergency at Ashford Terrace.

Question 50 is based on the following passage:

Police often ask eyewitnesses to identify a suspect from a lineup or an array of photos. A lineup or photo array involves placing a suspect or a photo of a suspect among people who are not suspected of committing the crime (fillers) and asking the eyewitness to identify the perpetrator. Misidentification by eyewitnesses has played a role in a high number of wrongful convictions and has led criminal justice experts to look more closely at the effectiveness of identifying suspects from live and photographic lineups.

50. Based on the preceding passage, which of the following statements is most accurate?
a. A photo array may contain only people who are not suspected of committing the crime.
b. The effectiveness of police lineups has been called into question recently.
c. A filler may have committed the crime.
d. The perpetrator will be asked to identify the criminal from a lineup.

Question 51 is based on the following passage:

When deciding to use less-lethal equipment, officers consider the circumstances and their agency's policy. Almost all larger law enforcement agencies have written policies about the use of less-lethal force. As part of their policy, agencies often have an approved use-of-force continuum to help officers decide the suitable amount of force for a situation — higher levels of force in the most severe circumstances, and less force in other circumstances. Many agencies in which officers use less-lethal technologies have training programs to help evaluate dangerous circumstances.

51. Based on the preceding passage, which of the following statements is most accurate?
a. Law enforcement agencies should give their officers clear instructions about the appropriate level of force for different situations.
b. The decision to use less-lethal equipment is entirely left to the officer on the scene.
c. Every law enforcement agency has a written policy about the use of less-lethal force.
d. Less-lethal force should be used in the most dangerous situations.

Question 52 is based on the following passage:

> Investigators often need to examine or verify the authenticity of a document that could be used as evidence in court or as aid in an investigation. Such documents are known as "questioned documents." Through visual examination or advanced chemical analysis of inks and paper, forensic investigators can determine information relating to a questioned document's authentication, authorship, or creation date. Such documents, printed or handwritten, could include checks, criminal confessions, counterfeit money, journal entries, threatening letters, or wills.

52. Based on the preceding passage, which of the following statements is most accurate?
    a. Most questioned documents are forged.
    b. A questioned document must be authenticated before it can be used legally.
    c. The authentication of questioned documents can take years.
    d. A questioned document can never be fully authenticated.

Questions 53 and 54 are based on the following passage:

> Racial profiling by law enforcement is commonly defined as a practice that targets people for suspicion of crime based on their race, ethnicity, religion, or national origin. Creating a profile about the kinds of people who commit certain types of crimes may lead officers to generalize about a particular group and act according to the generalization rather than specific behavior.
>
> Racial profiling can cause multiple problems. Several law enforcement agencies have gone through expensive litigation over civil rights concerns. Police-citizen relations in those communities have been strained, making policing all the more challenging. Most important, racial profiling is unlikely to be an effective policing strategy, as criminals can simply shift their activities outside the profile (e.g., if racial profiling begins with police stopping black males in their teens and twenties for being drug carriers, criminals may start using other demographic groups — such as Hispanics, children, or the elderly — to move drugs). Despite training to avoid discrimination, officers may still rely on cultural stereotypes and act on their perceptions of a person's characteristics (such as age, race, or gender).

53. Based on the preceding passage, which of the following statements is most accurate?
    a. The elderly are often the targets of racial profiling.
    b. Racial profiling only applies to African-Americans.
    c. The worst consequence of racial profiling is expensive litigation for law enforcement departments.
    d. Racial profiling may prevent a police officer from properly assessing a situation.

54. Based on the preceding passage, which of the following statements is most accurate?
    a. Racial profiling is more common in diverse areas.
    b. Anti-discrimination training has not been able to totally eradicate racial profiling.
    c. Criminals cannot adapt to racial profiling.
    d. Racial profiling is based on statistical data.

Question 55 is based on the following passage:
Social disorganization theory suggests that crime occurs when community relationships and local institutions fail or are absent. For example, a neighborhood with high residential turnover might have more crime than a neighborhood with a stable residential community.

55. Based on the preceding passage, which of the following statements is most accurate?
    a. Social disorganization theory would likely recommend efforts to improve community relationships.
    b. Social disorganization theory does not apply to urban areas.
    c. Social disorganization theory places the responsibility for crime on residents.
    d. Social disorganization theory has been proven false.

Questions 56 and 57 are based on the following passage:
Federal legislation allows U.S. Attorneys to enhance the penalty for crimes committed by gang members. A growing number of states have passed or are considering passing similar enhanced prosecution legislation. In practice, it is challenging to prove that an offender is a member of a gang or that the crime benefits the gang; therefore, it can be difficult to bring enhancement to bear on prosecuting criminal activity.

California, which leads the nation in the trend to enhance prosecution, describes the process this way: "any person who is convicted of a felony committed for the benefit of, at the direction of, or in association with any criminal street gang, with the specific intent to promote, further, or assist in any criminal conduct by gang members, shall, upon conviction of that felony, in addition and consecutive to the punishment prescribed for the felony," become subject to additional terms, enumerated in the code. Guidance is provided under the California code for persons convicted of misdemeanor offenses.

56. Based on the preceding passage, which of the following statements is most accurate?
    a. Only states can enhance penalties because of gang membership.
    b. Enhanced prosecution for gang members requires proof of gang membership.
    c. Only California has passed enhanced prosecution legislation.
    d. There are separate enhanced prosecution laws for repeat offenders.

57. Based on the preceding passage, which of the following statements is most accurate?
    a. Crimes associated with gang activity are subject to harsher penalties in California.
    b. Enhanced prosecution laws may apply to acts that are contrary to the gang's interests.
    c. Misdemeanors are not subject to enhanced prosecution in California.
    d. Gang members who commit crimes unrelated to their gang's activity may still be subject to enhanced prosecution.

Questions 58 and 59 are based on the following passage:

> Stalking can be carried out in person or via electronic mechanisms (phone, fax, GPS, cameras, computer spyware, or the Internet). Cyberstalking – the use of technology to stalk victims – shares some characteristics with real-life stalking. It involves the pursuit, harassment, or contact of others in an unsolicited fashion initially via the Internet and email. Cyberstalking can intensify in chat rooms where stalkers systematically flood their target's inbox with obscene, hateful, or threatening messages and images. A cyberstalker may further assume the identity of his or her victim by posting information (fictitious or not) and soliciting responses from the cybercommunity. Cyberstalkers may use information acquired online to further intimidate, harass, and threaten their victim via mail, phone calls, and physically appearing at a residence or workplace.

58. Based on the preceding passage, which of the following statements is most accurate?
    a. Cyberstalking may include impersonating the victim.
    b. Cyberstalking is identical to real-life stalking.
    c. Cyberstalking is the most common form of stalking at present.
    d. Cyberstalking rarely leads to real-life stalking.

59. Based on the preceding passage, which of the following statements is most accurate?
    a. Cyberstalking is primarily perpetrated by women.
    b. Episodes of cyberstalking are usually initiated by the victim.
    c. Cyberstalking is unsolicited by the victim.
    d. There is no connection between cyberstalking and other forms of stalking.

Questions 60 and 61 are based on the information listed below:

Restorative justice principles offer more inclusive processes and reorient the goals of justice. Restorative justice has been finding a receptive audience, as it creates common ground that accommodates the goals of many constituencies and provides a collective focus. The guiding principles of restorative justice are:

1. Crime is an offense against human relationships.
2. Victims and the community are central to justice processes.
3. The first priority of justice processes is to assist victims.
4. The second priority is to restore the community, to the degree possible.
5. The offender has personal responsibility to victims and to the community for crimes committed.
6. Stakeholders share responsibilities for restorative justice through partnerships for action.
7. The offender will develop improved competency and understanding as a result of the restorative justice experience.

60. Based on the preceding passage, which of the following statements is most accurate?
    a. Restorative justice is based on a close reading of the Constitution.
    b. The first priority in justice is to arrest criminals, according to the restorative justice model.
    c. In the restorative justice model, criminals should get nothing out of the process of justice.
    d. Restorative justice suggests that offenders owe something to the community.

61. Based on the preceding passage, which of the following statements is most accurate?
    a. Restorative justice requires the cooperation of all parties concerned.
    b. Restorative justice is most appropriate for juvenile offenders.
    c. The restorative justice model promotes changes in the sentencing process.
    d. Restorative justice focuses on criminal rehabilitation.

Questions 62 and 63 are based on the following passage:

The political turmoil of the twenty-first century and advances in technology make transnational crime a concern for the United States. Increased travel and trade and advances in telecommunications and computer technology have had the unintended effect of providing avenues for the rapid expansion of transnational organized crime activities. Policing objectives in the United States must extend beyond national borders to seek out and target this type of crime. Only through international collaboration and information exchange can the United States develop effective protocol and policies for countering these crimes and mount a serious opposition.

62. Based on the preceding passage, which of the following statements is most accurate?
    a. Transnational crime only occurs within the United States.
    b. Transnational crime is more prevalent than domestic crime.
    c. There should be an international organization for fighting transnational crime.
    d. The rise of transnational crime has been fueled by the Internet.

63. Based on the preceding passage, which of the following statements is most accurate?
    a. Advances in computer technology have benefited criminal organizations only.
    b. The United States will need the help of other nations in fighting transnational crime.
    c. The United States currently has an effective system for fighting transnational crime.
    d. Transnational crime could be eliminated by stricter customs enforcement.

Questions 64 and 65 are based on the following passage:
    Fraud is the intentional misrepresentation of information or identity to deceive others, the unlawful use of a credit or debit card or ATM, or the use of electronic means to transmit deceptive information, in order to obtain money or other things of value. Fraud may be committed by someone inside or outside the business. Fraud includes instances in which a computer was used to defraud the business of money, property, financial documents, insurance policies, deeds, use of rental cars, or various services by forgery, misrepresented identity, credit card or wire fraud. The legal definition of fraud excludes incidents of embezzlement.

64. Based on the preceding passage, which of the following statements is most accurate?
    a. Fraud is committed to obtain things of value.
    b. Fraud can only be committed by an employee.
    c. Today, most fraud involves the use of a computer.
    d. The owner of a business cannot commit fraud.

65. Based on the preceding passage, which of the following statements is most accurate?
    a. Most fraud involves the use of an ATM.
    b. Unintentional deception can still be prosecuted as fraud.
    c. Embezzlement is not considered fraud under the definition of the law.
    d. Forgery is the most common form of fraud.

Cloze

(66) _ _ _ _ _ 1974, it was believed that the maximum-security prison in Deloitte, Wisconsin was impossible (67) _ _ escape. However, in that (68) _ _ _ _ two cunning prisoners used a set of handmade tools to prove that (69) _ _ _ _ the best efforts of law enforcement could be undone (70) _ _ _ _ enough ingenuity, patience, and effort.

David Jackson and Fred Taylor had both been serving (71) _ _ _ _ sentences for murder in 1974. They were in the (72) _ _ _ _ cell block, and they also saw each other during their exercise time in (73) _ _ _ prison yard. Over their years together, (74) _ _ _ _ conceived of a plan to tunnel out of the prison through the (75) _ _ _ _ _ of the basement.

In order (76) _ _ _ this plan to work, however, the men needed to have a quality set of tools and regular access to the basement of the prison. Luckily for (77) _ _ _ _, the prison metal shop was located in the basement, and a few prisoners (78) _ _ _ _ allowed to work there as a reward for (79) _ _ _ _ behavior. Jackson and Taylor (80) _ _ _ _ sure to follow all of the prison rules, and within a few months they were both able to secure jobs in the metal (81) _ _ _ _.

At that point, they (82) _ _ _ access to all of the tools they would need to cut a hole (83) _ _ _ _ _ _ _ the floor of the prison basement. However, they had to figure out a (84) _ _ _ to steal these tools so that the guards (85) wouldn't know they were missing. Taylor was the one who (86) _ _ _ _ _ _ this problem. He figured (87) _ _ _ that by falsifying the metal shop's repair records, he could make it seem as (88) _ _ tools had broken and been discarded, (89) _ _ _ _ in fact they had been hidden elsewhere by Jackson and Taylor. Once the men had acquired enough tools to do the (90) _ _ _, they began slowly chipping away at the floor whenever they (91) _ _ _ a chance.

It took months for the two (92) _ _ _ to break through the cement floor, but once they had done this it appears that the work went much faster. They used shovels and pickaxes to (93) _ _ _ a tunnel under the northeastern wall of the prison complex, and they agreed to (94) _ _ _ _ until summer to escape, because they believed that the denser foliage in the woods around the prison would make it easier for them to evade capture in the hours after the breakout.

Finally, on July 13, 1974, Jackson and Taylor (95) _ _ _ _ their move. They emerged from the ground about a hundred yards (96) _ _ _ _ the prison wall, and immediately ran into the woods, (97) _ _ _ _ _ they changed into a set of civilian clothes they had stolen months before. Their escape was not noticed by the authorities (98) _ _ _ _ _ four hours later.

The escape of David Jackson and Fred Taylor made the national newspapers, (99) ___ hugely embarrassed prison officials, (100) ___ had previously claimed that their facility was escape-proof. However, the story did not (101) ___ happily for the two men. Jackson was apprehended two weeks (102) _____ while trying to cross the border into Canada, and Taylor was gunned down (103) __ police outside his ex-wife's house five days after Jackson was captured. Still, this prison escape will go down in history as one of the (104) ____ daring and unlikely in United (105) _____ history.

Reasoning

Instructions: Officers often face situations in which they need to determine how different pieces of information relate to one another. In this section, you will be presented with information such as a group or ordered series of facts, numbers, letters, or words. Your task is to study the various pieces of information and try to understand how they relate to one another. Mark the letter that identifies your choice on your answer sheet.

106. Identify the next number in the series: 12, 19, 26...
   a. 31
   b. 33
   c. 35
   d. 37

107. Three of the following words are similar, while one is different. Select the one that is different.
   a. elect
   b. candidate
   c. office-holder
   d. ballot

108. In the past year, Kevin made seven more arrests than Leonard, who made six more arrests than Mike. Nelson made ten more arrests than Mike. Who made the most arrests?
   a. Kevin
   b. Leonard
   c. Mike
   d. Nelson

109. Darren and Felix play in a basketball game. Darren scores three times as many points as Felix, who scores eight more than his average. How many points does Darren score?
   a. 8
   b. 9
   c. 24
   d. Not enough information

110. Identify the next number in the series: 7, 8, 9, 7, 8, 9, 7...
   a. 7
   b. 8
   c. 9
   d. 10

111. Three of the following things are similar, while one is different. Select the one that is different.
    a. fork
    b. spoon
    c. pan
    d. knife

112. Identify the next number in the series: 10, 21, 33, 46, 60…
    a. 72
    b. 73
    c. 74
    d. 75

113. Jake, Kevin, and Larry play on a basketball team. Jake scores 30 points, twice as many as Kevin. Larry scores ten more points than Kevin. How many points did Kevin score?
    a. 10
    b. 25
    c. 40
    d. Not enough information

114. Identify the next number in the series: 2, 5, 7, 8, 7, 5…
    a. 0
    b. 2
    c. 5
    d. 7

115. Lily, Marigold, and Charles are playing a game. Lily scores three more points than Marigold, who scores five fewer points than Charles. Who scored the most points?
    a. Charles
    b. Marigold
    c. Lily
    d. Not enough information

116. Identify the next number in the series: 40, 20, 10…
    a. 0
    b. 5
    c. 7
    d. 15

117. Three of the following words are similar, while one is different. Select the one that is different.
    a. smile
    b. fear
    c. sadness
    d. joy

118. Identify the next number in the series: 23, 21, 19, 17, 23, 21, 19, 17, 23...
    a. 17
    b. 19
    c. 21
    d. 23

119. Rosemary, Violet, Anya, and Snowflake run in a horse race. Rosemary finishes in between Anya and Snowflake, who finished in that order. Anya beats Violet, and Violet beats Snowflake. Which horse won the race?
    a. Anya
    b. Rosemary
    c. Violet
    d. Snowflake

120. Identify the next number in the series: 145, 451, 514...
    a. 0
    b. 145
    c. 154
    d. 415

121. Three of the following words are similar, while one is different. Select the one that is different.
    a. four
    b. seventh
    c. first
    d. ninth

Answers and Explanations #3

Clarity

1. A: In the other version, the conjunction plus is used incorrectly. The writer is describing a relationship between two different things: crime and violent imagery. The conjunction plus would lump these two things together, rather than keeping them separate so that they may be compared. In the correct version of the sentence, the terms are kept apart and the meaning is preserved.

2. B: The other version of the sentence suggests that the recruits, rather than the desks, are along the back wall of the room. By placing the location of the desks in an introductory clause, the correct version makes the location plain.

3. A: The other version of the sentence is unnecessarily wordy. The phrase "come to a decision" can be condensed to "decide" without any change in the meaning.

4. B: The other version is unclear because it is hard to tell to whom *he* refers. One might suppose that it refers to Sterling, because he was mentioned first, but this cannot be guaranteed. The correct version substitutes the name for the pronoun he, and thus becomes clearer.

5. A: The other version of the sentence is grammatically correct, but it does not do a good job of emphasizing the most important information in the sentence: the attack on the victim. In the correct version of the sentence, the route taken by the victim is placed in an introductory subordinate clause, which encourages the reader to focus more on the information contained in the main clause. This is a subtle distinction, but a good writer will be able to draw the reader's attention to the most important parts of the text.

6. B: The other version of the sentence confuses the comparison. Because "that of" is omitted, it sounds as if Chandra's investigative work is better than the other detectives themselves, rather than the work of those detectives. In the correct version, the terms of the comparison are clear.

7. A: In the other version, the conjunction *and* is used incorrectly. When the phrase "not only" is used at the beginning of a list (in this case, a list of the things included in a productive day), the second term in the list should be preceded by *but*.

8. A: In the other version, the verb tenses are inconsistent: *reading* and *playing* are gerunds (they end in *–ing*), while *take* is just in present tense.

9. B: In the other version, it cannot be determined whether she met the women occasionally, or whether they occasionally asked her about her haircut. The correct version positions the adverb so that this meaning is clear.

10. B: The other version is too wordy: it is not necessary to write "would be in violation of" when "would violate" conveys the same meaning.

11. B: In the other version, it sounds as if the car was driving itself. Although a reader would most likely be able to make sense of this statement, the introductory clause creates unnecessary confusion. In the correct version, the driver is properly identified.

12. A: The other sentence is redundant: when the sentence begins with *even though*, it is not necessary to include *yet* as well. Another way to correct this sentence would be, "Even though Frank had lived there all his life, he did not know the suspect."

13. A: In the other version, the subject and verb disagree: the subject is singular (one) and the verb is plural (feel). Note that the subject is singular, even though it includes a plural noun (students).

14. B: In the other version of the sentence, it is unclear whether the officers or the citizens worked near the police station. Both of the items in the series should be introduced with the pronoun who in order for the meaning to be clear.

15. A: The other version of the sentence has an inconsistent structure. The sentence includes a list (things the teacher asked John about). In the correct version, every item in the list is introduced with if, while in the incorrect version both if and did are used to introduce the items. The sentence is easier to read when the items in the list are introduced in the same way.

Spelling

16. D: noticeable

17. B: possession

18. A: library

19. B: until

20. B: questionnaire

21. A: recommend

22. C: restaurant

23. C: exercise

24. A: tongue

25. A: disappoint

26. B: incidentally

27. C: scissors

28. B: preferable

29. A: parallel

30. B: thorough

Vocabulary

31. D: *Understandable* most nearly has the same meaning as *coherent*. Both of them mean clear or easy to comprehend.

32. B: *Undermine* most nearly has the same meaning as *subvert*. Both of these words mean to destroy or to rebel against authority.

33. C: *Extend* most nearly has the same meaning as *protract*. Both of these words mean to make longer, whether in physical length or duration.

34. C: *Perpetrator* most nearly has the same meaning as *culprit*. Both of these words refer to criminals or wrongdoers.

35. A: *Meddle* most nearly has the same meaning as *interfere*. Both of these verbs mean to come between or to intervene.

36. B: *Plentiful* most nearly has the same meaning as *abundant*. Both of them mean in great supply.

37. D: *Impose* most nearly has the same meaning as *levy*. Both of these words mean apply or subject to.

38. B: *Satisfy* most nearly has the same meaning as *appease*. Both of these words mean to make right or to give enough to.

39. C: *Friendly* most nearly has the same meaning as *amiable*. Both of these words mean nice to other people or animals.

40. A: *Betray* most nearly has the same meaning as *forsake*. Both of these verbs refer to acts of cruelty to supposed friends.

41. B: *Compassion* most nearly has the same meaning as *empathy*. Both of these words mean concern or care for others.

42. B: *Replicate* most nearly has the same meaning as *duplicate*. Both of these verbs mean copy or mimic.

43. A: *Timely* most nearly has the same meaning as *punctual*. Both of these words mean on time or exercising good timing.

44. C: *Hatred* most nearly has the same meaning as *animosity*. Both of these words refer to anger towards another person.

45. B: *Disprove* most nearly has the same meaning as *rebut*. Both of these words mean to argue against, contradict, or prove wrong.

Reading Comprehension

46. A: Based on the passage, the most accurate statement is that crime tends to occur more often in particular areas. According to the second sentence, "it is clustered in small areas." The passage states that incidents of driving under the influence are more common not along main roads, but "in areas with a large number of bars or liquor stores." The passage never states that Minneapolis police ignored much of the city, only that their work was largely concentrated on a small number of places. Finally, the passage states that residential burglaries usually occur during daytime hours.

47. D: Based on the passage, the most accurate statement is that some times and places require more attention from police. These hot spots have been demonstrated to have more criminal activity. The passage does not, however, state that police should open stations in hot spots: there may be more effective ways to handle these problems. The passage states that assault, not public disorder, usually occurs between three and seven in the morning. In addition, assaults are more likely to occur when few other people are around.

48. A: Using the above coding system, the call number F-2-1 would signify an urgent public intoxication incident at Shackleford Banks.

49. A: Using the above coding system, the call number B-2-5 would signify an urgent burglary incident at Government Plaza.

50. B: Based on the passage, the most accurate statement is that the effectiveness of police lineups has been called into question recently. According to the final sentence, false convictions have undermined faith in traditional methods of identifying suspects. A photo array, meanwhile, will contain one suspect and several non-suspects, or fillers. These fillers are people who are not suspected of having committed the crime. Finally, the witness, and not the perpetrator, will be asked to identify the criminal from a lineup.

51. A: Based on the passage, the most accurate statement is that law enforcement agencies should give their officers clear instructions about the appropriate level of force for different situations. This is the main idea of the passage, and is expressed in every sentence. The decision about using less-lethal equipment is ideally a combination of the officer's assessment of the situation and the policy of the department. The passage states that "almost all larger law enforcement agencies have written policies," but clearly not all do. Finally, the passage states that officers will use "higher levels of force in the most severe circumstances, and less force in other circumstances."

52. B: Based on the passage, the most accurate statement is that a questioned document must be authenticated before it can be used legally. This is stated directly in the first sentence. Some questioned documents are forged, but the passage does not state that most are. The passage does not state that the authentication process can take years, or that it is impossible to ever fully authenticate a questioned document.

53. D: Based on the passage, the most accurate statement is that racial profiling may prevent a police officer from properly assessing a situation. The passage does not suggest that the elderly are often the targets of racial profiling, and indeed this would not really make sense. Similarly, there is no indication that racial profiling only applies to African-Americans, though the passage does suggest that African-Americans are subject to profiling. Expensive litigation may be a negative consequence of racial profiling, but it is by no means the worst.

54. B: Based on the passage, the most accurate statement is that anti-discrimination training has not been able to totally eradicate racial profiling. This fact is expressed in the final sentence of the passage. It seems possible that racial profiling is more common in diverse areas, but this is not expressed in the passage. The second paragraph describes how criminals will adapt quickly to racial profiling. Finally, the passage does not state that racial profiling is based on statistical data.

55. A: Based on the passage, the most accurate statement is that social disorganization theory would likely recommend efforts to improve community relationships. After all, this theory posits that poor relationships in the community contribute to increased crime. This theory clearly applies to urban areas and rural areas alike, and though it does suggest that the behavior of residents is an important factor in crime, the passage does not suggest that residents bear the responsibility. Finally, the passage does not indicate whether social disorganization theory has been accepted or proven false.

56. B: Based on the passage, the most accurate statement is that enhanced prosecution for gang members requires proof of gang membership. The first paragraph mentions that it can be difficult for attorneys to generate this proof. It is not true that only states can enhance prosecution: the first paragraph describes federal legislation that makes it possible for U.S. Attorneys to enhance interrogation. The second sentence of the first paragraph indicates that states besides California have passed enhanced prosecution legislation. The passage does not indicate that there are separate enhanced prosecution laws for repeat offenders.

57. A: Based on the passage, the most accurate statement is that crimes associated with gang activity are subject to harsher penalties in California. This is stated in the first sentence of the second paragraph. The passage makes clear that only acts that promote gang interests are subject to enhanced prosecution: in other words, unrelated crimes or crimes that are contrary to the gang's interests are not considered. The last sentence of the second paragraph indicates that misdemeanor offenses may also be subject to enhanced prosecution in California.

58. A: Based on the passage, the most accurate statement is that cyberstalking may include impersonating the victim. The passage states this directly: "A cyberstalker may further assume the identity of his or her victim..." The passage makes clear that cyberstalking "shares some characteristics with real-life stalking," but is not identical. The passage does not state that cyberstalking is the most common form of stalking at present, though it may be assumed that it is becoming more common. Finally, the passage does not indicate that

- 136 -

cyberstalking rarely leads to real-life stalking; on the contrary, the final sentence suggests that this is not an uncommon occurrence.

59. C: Based on the passage, the most accurate statement is that cyberstalking is unsolicited by the victim. The third sentence states that cyberstalking "involves the pursuit, harassment, or contact of others in an unsolicited fashion." There is no suggestion that cyberstalking is primarily perpetrated by women, though this seems unlikely. Furthermore, the passage does not indicate that most episodes of cyberstalking are initiated by the victim, though this also seems improbable. Finally, the passage makes plain in the second sentence that cyberstalking "shares some characteristics with real-life stalking."

60. D: Based on the passage, the most accurate statement is that restorative justice suggests that offenders owe something to the community. This is stated directly in the fifth item of the list. There is no suggestion in the passage that restorative justice is based on a close reading of the Constitution. The restorative justice model identifies assisting victims, not arresting criminals, as the first priority in restorative justice. Restorative justice does assert that the offender should develop "improved competency and understanding" out of the justice process.

61. A: Based on the passage, the most accurate statement is that restorative justice requires the cooperation of all parties concerned. This is clear in the sixth item of the list: "Stakeholders share responsibilities for restorative justice through partnerships for action." There is no indication that this model of justice is most appropriate for juvenile offenders, or that it promotes changes in the sentencing process. Criminal rehabilitation is part of the restorative justice model, but it is not necessarily the focus.

62. D: Based on the passage, the most accurate statement is that the rise of transnational crime has been fueled by the Internet. The passage suggests this in the first sentence ("advances in technology make transnational crime a concern") and further elaborates it in the second. Transnational crime, by definition, occurs across national borders. The passage does not state that transnational crime is more prevalent than domestic crime. The passage argues that there should be greater cooperation between nations in the fight against transnational crime, but does not state that there should be an international organization for fighting transnational crime.

63. B: Based on the passage, the most accurate statement is that the United States will need the help of other nations in fighting transnational crime. The final sentence states that "only through international collaboration" can the United States be effective in fighting these crimes. The passage does not state that advances in computer technology have benefited criminal organizations only, and it may be assumed that these advances have also aided investigation and prosecution efforts. It seems clear that the United States does not have an effective system for fighting transnational crime at present, and there is no indication in the passage that stricter customs enforcement could eliminate this problem.

64. A: Based on the passage, the most accurate statement is that fraud is committed to obtain things of value. The first sentence of the passage defines fraud as any of a number of

deceptions committed "to obtain money or other things of value." The passage does not suggest that fraud can only be committed by an employee, and, indeed, it directly states that "fraud may be committed by someone inside or outside the business." The passage does not state that most fraud today involves the use of a computer, though it does indicate that computers are often used in fraud. Finally, the passage never states that the owner of a business cannot commit fraud. On the contrary, the definition of the crime suggests that it may be committed by any person in any position.

65. C: Based on the passage, the most accurate statement is that embezzlement is not considered fraud under the definition of the law. This is stated explicitly in the last sentence. The passage does not suggest that forgery is the most common form of fraud, or that most fraud involves the use of an ATM, though both of these scenarios are listed as forms of fraud. The passage states that fraud must be an intentional misrepresentation, so it would seem that unintentional deception could not be prosecuted as fraud.

Cloze

66. until

67. two

68. year

69. even

70. with

71. life

72. same

73. the

74. they

75. floor

76. for

77. them

78. were

79. good

80. were

81. shop

82. had

83. through

84. way

85. wouldn't

86. solved

87. out

88. if

89. when

90. job

91. had

92. men

93. dig

94. wait

95. made

96. from

97. where

98. until

99. and

100. who

101. end

102. later

103. by

104. most

105. States

Reasoning

106. B: The next number in the series is 33. In this series, the numbers increase by seven each time.

107. A: The word *elect* is not like the other three. *Candidate*, *office-holder*, and *ballot* are all nouns related to voting and democracy, while *elect* is a verb.

108. A: Kevin has made the most arrests. If Kevin made seven more arrests than Leonard, who made six more than Mike, then Kevin made thirteen more than Mike. Therefore, Kevin also made three more than Nelson.

109. C: There is not enough information to solve this problem. Felix's average point total is not given, so it is impossible to calculate Darren's point total for the game.

110. B: The next number in the series is 8. This pattern is just recurring groups of three numbers: 7, 8, and 9. So, after each 7 would come an 8.

111. C: A pan is not like the other three things. Forks, spoons, and knives are all eating utensils, but a pan is not.

112. D: The next number in the series is 75. The difference between the terms in this series increases by one with each successive term.

113. B: Kevin scored 25 points. If Jake scored 30 points, and this was twice as many as Kevin, then Kevin scored 15. Larry, then, scored 10 more points than Kevin.

114. B: The next number in the series is 2. This series is symmetrical: that is, it increases to 8 and then retraces its steps back down to 2.

115. A: Charles scored the most points. If Lily scored three more than Marigold and five fewer than Charles, then Charles must have scored two more points than Lily.

116. B: The next number in the series is 5. In this series, each number is half of the previous number. Another way to express this would be that the next number in the series can be found by dividing the last number by 2.

117. A: The word *smile* is not like the other three. Fear, sadness, and joy are all emotions, while a smile is merely a gesture, or the sign of an emotion.

118. C: The next number in the series is 21. In this pattern, the four numbers 23, 21, 19 and 17 repeat over and over again. So, after the 23 would come a 21.

119. A: Anya won the race. Since Rosemary finished in between Anya and Snowflake, then neither Rosemary nor Snowflake won the race. If Anya beat Violet, then Violet did not win either, meaning that Anya must have won the race.

120. B: The next number in the series is 145. In this series, the digits of each number move forward one position, with the first number becoming the last. So, after 514 would come 145.

121. A: The word *four* is not like the other three. *Seventh*, *first*, and *ninth* are called ordinals, because they are used to describe the order in which items are placed. *Four*, however, simply names the number.

Practice Test #4

Clarity

Instructions: In the following pairs of sentences, identify the sentence that is most clearly written. If sentence "a" is more clear than sentence "b," mark "a" on your answer sheet. If sentence "b" is more clear than sentence "a," mark "b" on your answer sheet.

1.   a. Pedro began his shift by filling his service vehicle with gas and a cup of coffee.
       b. Pedro began his shift by filling his service vehicle with gas and buying a cup of coffee.

2.   a. The department budget is inflated now because of purchases like the new fax machine.
       b. The department budget is inflated at this point in time because of purchases along the lines of the new fax machine.

3.   a. Receiving the diploma, his instructor called Leonard the best student he had ever had.
       b. As Leonard received his diploma, his instructor called him his best student ever.

4.   a. He filled his notebook with interesting comments from the neighbors and onlookers while he was collecting evidence.
       b. Collecting evidence, his notebook filled with interesting comments from the neighbors and onlookers.

5.   a. The guys he ran into in the locker room sometimes bragged about their fancy cars.
       b. Sometimes, the guys he ran into in the locker room bragged about their fancy cars.

6.   a. Although the district is well funded overall, the police department lacks even the most basic supplies.
       b. Although the district is well funded overall, but the police department lacks even the most basic supplies.

7.   a. The protesters resisted the efforts of police to subdue them.
       b. The protesters were resistant to the efforts of police to subdue them.

8.   a. Citizens are advised to remain in their homes if possible until the situation has been resolved.
       b. Until the situation has been resolved, citizens are advised to if possible remain in their homes.

9.   a. I was working at the library when I heard the news about Trevor's acquittal.
b. I was doing homework at the library when I heard the news about Trevor's acquittal.

10.   a. Just when he thought it was over, Lonnie remembers his training and returns to the crime scene.
b. Just when he thought it was over, Lonnie remembered his training and returned to the crime scene.

11.   a. An effective supervisor knows when to ignore minor errors.
b. An effective supervisor knows when they need to ignore minor errors.

12.   a. The correct procedure for detaining a suspect was second nature to Kelly after she completed the training course.
b. After completing the training course, the correct procedure for detaining a suspect was second nature to Kelly.

13.   a. Government oversight is where elected officials examine the policies and actions of city employees, including the police department.
b. Government oversight is examination of the policies and actions of city employees, including the police department, by elected officials.

14.   a. The magazine journalists who cover law enforcement are much more fair-minded than the newspapers.
b. The magazine journalists who cover law enforcement are much more fair-minded than those of the newspapers.

15.   a. In the richest neighborhoods, all cars were not properly registered with the municipal department.
b. In the richest neighborhoods, not all cars were properly registered with the municipal department.

Spelling

Instructions: In the following sentences, choose the correct spelling of the missing word. Mark on your answer sheet the letter that identifies the correct choice.

16. "I _____ wish things had gone differently," she said with obvious regret.
    a. truely
    b. truly
    c. trooly
    d. trewly

17. The officer responded to a frantic call from a citizen, but when she arrived she found nothing more than some minor _____.
    a. mischief
    b. mischeff
    c. mischiff
    d. mischeif

18. Unless there is an immediate _____ in unnecessary spending, the project will be way over budget.
    a. reduckshen
    b. reduction
    c. reducton
    d. reducshen

19. His excellent performance in several subjects made him a natural _____ for the "Best All-Around Student" award.
    a. cadidate
    b. cannadate
    c. candidate
    d. cannidate

20. The mission would require a great deal of outdoor reconnaissance, so the team leader required all the soldiers to pack their _____ uniforms.
    a. camelflage
    b. camofladge
    c. camouflage
    d. camoflage

21. Frank did not break any bones in the accident, but his _____ was torn in several places.
    a. cartilage
    b. cartilege
    c. carrtiladge
    d. cartilige

22. The _____ story is that his car slipped out of gear and rolled downhill, but we all know that the truth is quite different.
    a. offishel
    b. official
    c. offishul
    d. offeshel

23. The printer offered a complete _____: if customers were not satisfied with the finished product, they could have their money back.
    a. guarantee
    b. garantee
    c. garauntee
    d. gaurantee

24. Once she learned how to operate the program, she began to _____ points at a steady pace.
    a. acumulate
    b. acummulate
    c. accumulate
    d. acumullate

25. She was looking forward to the end of the school year, when she could finally devote her full attention to developing her small _____.
    a. busyness
    b. bizzeness
    c. bussiness
    d. business

26. She loved coming home on the weekends, _____ when her brother and sister were in town as well.
    a. especially
    b. espeshelley
    c. aspicially
    d. espechelly

27. He was the first in his family to _____ in any sport, and his parents hardly knew how to react.
    a. axel
    b. excel
    c. axul
    d. axcel

28. Julian's background in _____ was a major advantage in his new laboratory job.
   a. science
   b. sience
   c. siunce
   d. scyence

29. She felt that she had run as well as she could, but she still only finished in _____ place.
   a. furth
   b. forth
   c. fourth
   d. fourfth

30. The situation was further complicated when it was discovered that the cans had not been _____ properly.
   a. labeled
   b. labelled
   c. labiled
   d. labelled

Vocabulary

Instructions: In each of the following sentences, choose the word or phrase that most nearly has the same meaning as the underlined word. Mark on your answer sheet the letter that identifies the correct choice.

31. His harsh manner managed to <u>aggravate</u> most of his coworkers within a few weeks.
    a. irritate
    b. allow
    c. debate
    d. announce

32. To <u>rectify</u> his mistake, he pledged an annual donation to the school's scholarship fund.
    a. alter
    b. correct
    c. ensnare
    d. delay

33. He was terrified that the other children would <u>humiliate</u> him because of his stutter.
    a. conquer
    b. embarrass
    c. ease
    d. placate

34. His pyramid scheme was perfectly organized to <u>bilk</u> senior citizens out of their life savings.
    a. feel
    b. establish
    c. offend
    d. con

35. Though he remained <u>supine</u>, from the couch he ordered his bodyguards to show the visitor out immediately.
    a. recumbent
    b. relaxed
    c. entire
    d. attentive

36. During his <u>descent</u> from the peak, the change in air pressure began to make him nauseous.
    a. expensive
    b. injured
    c. improper
    d. lowering

37. He was able to <u>surmount</u> every obstacle along the way, from bad weather to inconsistent equipment.
    a. continue
    b. overcome
    c. express
    d. select

38. The plan to <u>allocate</u> the funds equally was complicated by the absence of several key committee members.
    a. distribute
    b. enrapture
    c. ruin
    d. hoard

39. His quest for <u>redemption</u> began by repairing the property he had damaged.
    a. collection
    b. fascination
    c. collapse
    d. recovery

40. They could never fully explain the <u>rationale</u> behind their decision to move.
    a. continue
    b. encourage
    c. finish
    d. reason

41. He didn't request <u>remuneration</u>, but he was happy to accept it when it was offered.
    a. assembly
    b. payment
    c. entrapment
    d. flow

42. His best efforts were not enough to <u>supplant</u> Hector at the top of the tennis rankings.
    a. replace
    b. send out
    c. deny
    d. acknowledge

43. The <u>plaintiff</u> contended that Steve was behind the wheel when the mailbox was destroyed.
    a. subject
    b. container
    c. accuser
    d. declaration

44. He hoped to <u>incite</u> action with his impassioned speech.
   a. diminish
   b. encourage
   c. slant
   d. languish

45. The jury took only an hour before rendering its <u>decision</u>.
   a. address
   b. allowance
   c. summary
   d. verdict

Reading Comprehension

Instructions: Officers must read and understand a wide range of materials. This test is designed to measure your ability to read and understand various types of written material. Read each paragraph or passage and choose the statement that best answers the question. All questions pertain only to the material in the passage that precedes them. Choose your answer solely on the basis of the material contained in the passage. Mark the letter that identifies your choice in the space on your answer sheet. Do not spend too much time on any one item.

Questions 46 and 47 are based on the following passage:

Geography has a major influence on crime. The features and characteristics of cityscapes and rural landscapes can make it easier or more difficult for crime to occur. The placement of alleys, buildings, and open spaces, for example, affects the likelihood that a criminal will strike. Combining geographic data with police report data and then displaying the information on a map is an effective way to analyze where, how, and why crime occurs.

Computerized crime maps became more commonplace with the introduction of desktop computing and software programs called Geographic Information Systems (GIS). Analysts map where crime occurs, combine the resulting visual display with other geographic data (such as location of schools, parks, and industrial complexes), analyze and investigate the causes of crime, and develop responses. Recent advances in statistical analysis make it possible to add more geographic and social dimensions to the analysis.

46. Based on the preceding passage, which of the following statements is most accurate?
    a. Geographical data is more useful in urban areas.
    b. Criminals are more likely to strike in open areas.
    c. Geographical data can be very useful in law enforcement.
    d. Police report data is useless without geographical data.

47. Based on the preceding passage, which of the following statements is most accurate?
    a. Police have only recently begun using geographical data in their work.
    b. Technological innovation has further increased the utility of geographic data.
    c. Geographic Information Systems have reduced the crime rate.
    d. The causes of crime can all be attributed to geographic factors.

Questions 48 and 49 are based on the following passage:

It's a fact that certain kinds of activities can indicate terrorist plans that are in the works, especially when they occur at or near high-profile sites or places where large numbers of people gather – like government buildings, military facilities, utilities, bus or train stations, or major public events. If you see or know about suspicious activities, please report them immediately to the proper authorities. In the United States, that means your closest Joint Terrorist Task Force, located in an FBI Field Office. In other countries, that means your closest law enforcement/counterterrorism agency.

48. Based on the preceding passage, which of the following statements is most accurate?
    a. Public assistance is needed in the fight against terrorism.
    b. Other countries do not have effective counterterrorism organizations.
    c. Terrorists are usually more interested in unpopulated areas.
    d. Civilians should not be near military facilities under any circumstances.

49. Based on the preceding passage, which of the following statements is most accurate?
    a. Every FBI Field Office contains a Joint Terrorist Task Force.
    b. Some activities are more suspicious when they occur in particular places.
    c. Citizens should attempt to apprehend terrorism suspects on their own.
    d. A large number of people tend to gather at utility stations.

Question 50 is based on the following passage:

Crime pattern theory integrates crime within a geographic context that demonstrates how the environments people live in and pass through influence criminality. The theory specifically focuses on places and the lack of social control or other measures of guardianship that are informally needed to control crime. For example, a suburban neighborhood can become a hot spot for burglaries because some homes have inadequate protection and nobody home to guard the property.

50. Based on the preceding passage, which of the following statements is most accurate?
    a. Crime pattern theory is only concerned with suburban crime.
    b. Crime pattern theory places the responsibility for crime on the neighborhood watch.
    c. Crime pattern theory focuses on the relationship between crime and place.
    d. Crime pattern theory applies only to minor offenses, like burglary.

Questions 51 and 52 are based on the following passage:

One of the most common forms of evidence investigators may detect and collect at a crime scene is impression and pattern evidence.

Impression evidence is created when two objects come in contact with enough force to cause an "impression." Typically impression evidence is either two-dimensional — such as a fingerprint — or three-dimensional — such as the marks on a bullet caused by the barrel of a firearm.

Pattern evidence may be additional identifiable information found within an impression. For example, an examiner will compare shoeprint evidence with several shoe-sole patterns to identify a particular brand, model, or size. If a shoe recovered from a suspect matches this initial pattern, the forensic examiner can look for unique characteristics that are common between the shoe and the shoeprint, such as tread wear, cuts, or nicks.

51. Based on the preceding passage, which of the following statements is most accurate?
    a. Impression evidence is more valuable than pattern evidence.
    b. Shoes are the most common source of pattern evidence.
    c. A footprint on a carpet would be an example of impression evidence.
    d. Pattern evidence must be verified by a state laboratory before it can be admitted for trial.

52. Based on the preceding passage, which of the following statements is most accurate?
    a. Forensic examiners can match a shoe to a shoe print.
    b. Pattern evidence requires less analysis than impression evidence.
    c. A left shoe cannot be matched to a right shoe print.
    d. A shoe print is not enough evidence to generate a conviction.

Question 53 is based on the following passage:

The broken windows theory explains how lesser crimes, untended areas, blight, graffiti, and signs of disorder decrease neighborhood residents' willingness to enforce social order, which in turn leads to more serious crime. If police target minor transgressions, they may prevent serious crime from developing in those places.

53. Based on the preceding passage, which of the following statements is most accurate?
    a. The broken windows theory would explain crime in wealthy neighborhoods.
    b. According to the broken windows theory, vandalism is the worst crime.
    c. The broken windows theory does not apply to rural areas.
    d. The broken windows theory draws a link between minor and major crimes.

Questions 54 and 55 are based on the following passage:

Current research finds that the management and culture of a department are the most important factors influencing police behavior. How the department is managed will dramatically affect how officers behave toward citizens. And how officers behave toward citizens will affect whether citizens view law enforcement as an institution with integrity.

Organizations that place priorities in the following areas will do better at maintaining integrity: accountability of managers and supervisors; equal treatment for all members of the organization; citizen accessibility to the department; inspections and audits; and quality education for employees. Defining values and principles and incorporating them in every facet of operations may be more important than hiring decisions. Diligence in detecting and addressing misconduct will show officers that managers practice what they preach.

54. Based on the preceding passage, which of the following statements is most accurate?
    a. Departmental culture is separate from how officers interact with the public.
    b. Law enforcement departments should get recommendations from citizens.
    c. The primary factor influencing police behavior is the crime rate.
    d. Departmental culture has far-reaching effects in law enforcement.

55. Based on the preceding passage, which of the following statements is most accurate?
    a. An organization should have defined values and principles.
    b. Once organizational policies are in place, managers should be able to ignore them.
    c. Misconduct generally takes a long time to detect.
    d. Managers will receive preferential treatment in effective organizations.

Questions 56 and 57 are based on the information listed below:

Radio code is the coding system for identifying units both inside and outside the department. There are three components to every radio code. Each of these components must be included when officers are dispatched. In this coding system, units are identified with three characters: a letter designating the shift, a number designating the area, and a letter identifying the type of event.

Shift
A: Day
B: Swing
C: Graveyard

Area
0: Central
1: South
2: East
3: West
4: North

Event
A: Drug offense
B: Traffic violation
C: Disorderly conduct
D: Assault
E: Robbery
F: Vandalism

56. Using the above coding system, the call number C-4-A would signify:
    a. a drug offense in the northern part of the city during the day shift.
    b. a traffic violation in the southern part of the city during the swing shift.
    c. disorderly conduct in the western part of the city during the graveyard shift.
    d. an assault in the southern part of the city during the day shift.

57. Using the above coding system, the call number B-0-B would signify:
    a. disorderly conduct in the western part of the city during the graveyard shift.
    b. a traffic violation in the central part of the city during the swing shift.
    c. harassment in the eastern part of the city during the day shift.
    d. an assault in the western part of the city during the swing shift.

Question 58 is based on the following passage:

Transnational organized crime involves the planning and execution of illicit business ventures by groups or networks of individuals working in more than one country. These criminal groups use systematic violence and corruption to achieve their goals. Crimes commonly include money laundering, human smuggling, cybercrime, and trafficking of humans, drugs, weapons, endangered species, body parts, or nuclear material.

58. Based on the preceding passage, which of the following statements is most accurate?
    a. Transnational crime often involves smuggling contraband across national borders.
    b. Transnational crime is most common in Eastern Europe.
    c. Transnational crime is restricted to the Internet.
    d. Transnational crime is only a problem for the United States.

Question 59 is based on the following passage:

Evidence refers to information or objects that may be admitted into court for judges and juries to consider when hearing a case. Evidence can come from varied sources — from genetic material or trace chemicals to dental history or fingerprints. Evidence can serve many roles in an investigation, such as to trace an illicit substance, identify remains, or reconstruct a crime.

59. Based on the preceding passage, which of the following statements is most accurate?
    a. It is difficult to use dental history in a trial.
    b. Evidence does not need to be admitted into court to be considered by a jury.
    c. Only the prosecution may introduce evidence during a trial.
    d. Evidence does not have to be physical material.

Question 60 is based on the following passage:

People between the ages of 15 and 24 are most likely to be targeted by gun violence as opposed to other forms of violence. From 1976 to 2005, 77 percent of homicide victims ages 15-17 died from gun-related injuries. This age group was most at risk for gun violence during this time period. Teens and young adults are more likely than persons of other ages to be murdered with a gun. Most violent gun crime, especially homicide, occurs in cities and urban communities.

60. Based on the preceding passage, which of the following statements is most accurate?
    a. Young adults are more likely to commit acts of gun violence.
    b. Teenagers and young adults are more likely than other people to be the victims of gun violence.
    c. The leading cause of death among middle-aged citizens is not gun violence.
    d. Most gun violence occurs in rural areas.

Question 61 is based on the following passage:

Enduring stress for a long period of time can lead to anxiety, depression, or post-traumatic stress disorder (PTSD). PTSD is a psychological condition marked by an inability to be intimate, inability to sleep, increased nightmares, and increased feelings of guilt and reliving the event. For law enforcement officers, stress can increase fatigue to the point that decision making is impaired and officers cannot properly protect themselves or citizens.

61. Based on the preceding passage, which of the following statements is most accurate?
    a. Stress can be detrimental to an officer's performance.
    b. PTSD is associated with excessive sleeping.
    c. Most law enforcement officers suffer from fatigue.
    d. Depression can lead to stress.

Questions 62 and 63are based on the following passage:

Like domestic violence, stalking is a crime of power and control. Stalking is conservatively defined as "a course of conduct directed at a specific person that involves repeated (two or more occasions) visual or physical proximity, nonconsensual communication, or verbal, written, or implied threats, or a combination thereof, that would cause a reasonable person fear." Stalking behaviors also may include persistent patterns of leaving or sending the victim unwanted items or presents that may range from seemingly romantic to bizarre, following or lying in wait for the victim, damaging or threatening to damage the victim's property, defaming the victim's character, or harassing the victim via the Internet by posting personal information or spreading rumors about the victim.

62. Based on the preceding passage, which of the following statements is most accurate?
    a. Stalking does not occur unless a person is intending to stalk.
    b. Stalking and domestic violence are the same crime.
    c. Stalking requires physical proximity.
    d. Stalking must include multiple episodes.

63. Based on the preceding passage, which of the following statements is most accurate?
    a. Stalking requires verbal communication.
    b. Sending a person flowers could be part of a pattern of stalking.
    c. Most stalking goes unreported by the victims.
    d. Stalking may include physical violence against another person.

Questions 64 and 65 are based on the following passage:

Burglary is the unlawful or forcible entry or attempted entry of a residence. This crime usually, but not always, involves theft. The illegal entry may be by force, such as breaking a window or slashing a screen, or may be without force by entering through an unlocked door or an open window. As long as the person entering has no legal right to be present in the structure, a burglary has occurred.

Furthermore, the structure need not be the house itself for a burglary to take place; illegal entry of a garage, shed, or any other structure on the premises also constitutes household burglary. If breaking and entering occurs in a hotel or vacation residence, it is still classified as a burglary for the household whose member or members were staying there at the time the entry occurred.

64. Based on the preceding passage, which of the following statements is most accurate?
    a. Burglary rarely occurs at vacation residences.
    b. Burglary cannot occur at a hotel.
    c. Burglary always occurs when at a residence, even when that residence is not a home.
    d. There are situations in which burglary is lawful.

65. Based on the preceding passage, which of the following statements is most accurate?
    a. A burglar may have a legal right to the residence where the burglary occurs.
    b. Burglary without force is better than burglary with force.
    c. A burglary may be committed without a theft taking place.
    d. Breaking into a shed is considered burglary regardless of where the shed is located.

Cloze

The incident began (66) _ _ _ _ Mary heard a suspicious noise in the middle of the (67) _ _ _ _ _. There was a series (68) _ _ short, sharp bumps, and then her dog started barking. Except for the dog, Mary was (69) _ _ _ _ _ in the house, so naturally she was on guard (70) _ _ _ _ the start. Also, she had been having arguments (71) _ _ _ _ her ex-husband recently, and she worried that he might (72) _ _ _ _ been drinking. Her ex-husband's behavior could be erratic when he was (73) _ _ _ _ _, and he had even been violent with her on occasion.

With this in mind, Mary decided to (74) _ _ _ _ the police. She dialed 911 and the dispatcher (75) _ _ _ _ _ her about the problems. (76) _ _ _ _ _ Mary was on the phone, she (77) _ _ _ _ _ the noise a few more times. She couldn't (78) _ _ sure, but it sounded (79) _ _ _ _ it was getting closer. Her dog continued (80) _ _ bark. She gave the dispatcher her address, and was told that an officer (81) _ _ _ _ _ be at her house as (82) _ _ _ _ as possible.

Mary (83) _ _ _ _ up the phone. She called her (84) _ _ _, who was still growling and barking in the direction of the front (85) _ _ _ _, and brought him into the bedroom (86) _ _ _ _ her. Then, she locked the door and huddled down (87) _ _ _ _ _ the covers. She wasn't terrified: she was mainly hoping (88) _ _ _ _ her ex-husband wouldn't make a scene that would wake the neighbors.

It took about ten minutes (89) _ _ _ the police to arrive. During this period, Mary (90) _ _ _ _ _ the suspicious noise a few more times. She thought that perhaps it (91) _ _ _ getting louder, but she couldn't be certain. In (92) _ _ _ case, she was pleased when she saw the flashing lights of the squad (93) _ _ _ approach, and when the front doorbell rang, even though the sound of the bell made her dog bark even (94) _ _ _ _ furiously. She got out from under the covers and headed to the front (95) _ _ _ _.

The officer who had responded (96) _ _ Mary's call asked her to describe the noise. When Mary did so, he (97) _ _ _ _ that he had a hunch, pulled his large flashlight from his belt holster, and headed around the side of the (98) _ _ _ _ _. About ten seconds (99) _ _ _ _ _, he returned with a big grin. He asked Mary to come with him, and when (100) _ _ _ _ reached the side of the house, he shined his flashlight up at a large oak (101) _ _ _ _. Mary could see that a large branch had broken, and that the end of the (102) _ _ _ _ _ _ was swinging from the base. When the wind caught the branch, it bumped against the upstairs window of Mary's (103) _ _ _ _ _. Mary, a little embarrassed but (104) _ _ _ _ very relieved, thanked the officer and went back (105) _ _ _ _ her house, where she fell back asleep almost at once.

Reasoning

Instructions: Officers often face situations in which they need to determine how different pieces of information relate to one another. In this section, you will be presented with information such as a group or ordered series of facts, numbers, letters, or words. Your task is to study the various pieces of information and try to understand how they relate to one another. Mark the letter which identifies your choice on your answer sheet.

106. Identify the next number in the series: 11, 22, 33, 11, 22…
    a. 0
    b. 11
    c. 22
    d. 33

107. Three of the following words are similar, while one is different. Select the one that is different.
    a. think
    b. ate
    c. jumped
    d. ran

108. Identify the next number in the series: 4, 8, 16, 32…
    a. 36
    b. 48
    c. 64
    d. 72

109. Three of the following things are similar, while one is different. Select the one that is different.
    a. hamster
    b. cat
    c. snake
    d. bear

110. Sandra received a 92 on the exam, and Terry's score was seven points lower. Victor scored ten points higher than Terry. What was Victor's score?
    a. 75
    b. 85
    c. 92
    d. 95

111. Wanda is twice as old as Ursula, and Ursula is seven years older than Vicky. How old is Vicky?
    a. 12
    b. 18
    c. 22
    d. Not enough information

112. Identify the next number in the series: 23, 44, 23, 54, 23, 64...
    a. 23
    b. 64
    c. 74
    d. 84

113. Three of the following words are similar, while one is different. Select the one that is different.
    a. sip
    b. gulp
    c. drink
    d. gnaw

114. Andrew, Ben, Carl, and Dan were in a race. Andrew finished after Ben but before Carl. Dan finished in between Carl and Andrew. Who won the race?
    a. Andrew
    b. Ben
    c. Carl
    d. Dan

115. Identify the next number in the series: 4, 7, 10, 4, 7...
    a. 4
    b. 7
    c. 10
    d. Not enough information

116. Grace is three years younger than Nora, who is five years older than Melanie. Melanie is seventeen years old. How old is Grace?
    a. 19
    b. 20
    c. 21
    d. 22

117. Three of the following words are similar, while one is different. Select the one that is different.
    a. tree
    b. rock
    c. person
    d. flower

118. Identify the next number in the series: 673, 367, 736,
    a. 367
    b. 637
    c. 673
    d. 763

119. Ned, Oscar, and Paul are in a class. On one test, Ned scored an 85 and Oscar scored seven points higher. If Paul scored three points higher than Ned, what was Paul's score?
    a. 82
    b. 85
    c. 88
    d. 95

120. Identify the next number in the series: 98, 89, 77, 99, 90, 78, 100…
    a. 77
    b. 79
    c. 91
    d. 101

121. Three of the following words are similar, while one is different. Select the one that is different.
    a. tongue
    b. belt
    c. shoe
    d. hat

Answers and Explanations #4

Clarity

1. B: The other version fails to assign a verb to the second item in the list (that is, the list of things Pedro began his shift by doing), and thereby suggests that Pedro filled his service vehicle with a cup of coffee. In a list of this type, there must be appropriate verbs for each of the items.

2. A: The other version of the sentence is too wordy. Phrases like "at this point in time" and "along the lines of" make sense, but they inflate the sentence and make it more difficult for the reader. In the better version, "at this point in time" has been replaced by "now" and "along the lines of" has been replaced by "like," with no alteration in the meaning.

3. B: In the other version, it sounds as if the instructor rather than Leonard has received the diploma. The correct version makes this clear in the introductory clause. In addition, the incorrect version contains the wordy phrase "best student he had ever had," which can be expressed more precisely as "best student ever."

4. A: The other version is written as if the notebook was collecting the evidence. In the correct version, the subject is clear.

5. B: In the other version, it is impossible to tell whether sometimes refers to the guys in the locker room or the bragging. That is, the reader has no way of knowing whether the speaker sometimes saw these guys or they sometimes bragged about their cars. In the correct version, the meaning is plain.

6. A: The other version is incorrect because the word but is unnecessary and confusing. The introductory phrase, because it begins with "although," alerts the reader that the main part of the sentence will describe something that has happened in spite of the district funding. Therefore, the inclusion of but at the beginning of the main clause is redundant.

7. A: The other version is too wordy. There is no reason to use the phrase *were resistant to* when the same meaning can be conveyed by *resisted*.

8. A: The other version contains a split infinitive, which is a common grammatical error that can lead to confusion. An infinitive is the verb form to ___. In sentence B, the infinitive is *to remain*. The placement of the phrase if possible breaks up the verb and makes the sentence more awkward. This split infinitive does not alter the meaning of the sentence, but there are situations in which a split infinitive changes the meaning from what the writer intends. Whenever possible, split infinitives should be avoided.

9. B: In the other version, it is unclear whether the speaker is an employee of the library or he or she was doing some other work there. The correct version makes this clear.

10. B: The other version of the sentence is confusing because the verb tenses are inconsistent. The first verb (thought) is in the past tense, and the next two (remembers and returns) are in the present tense. In the correct version, all of the verbs are in the past tense.

11. A: In the other version, there is a disagreement between the subject (supervisor) and the pronoun later used to refer to it (they). It is common in conversation to use they in this way, but it is grammatically incorrect and makes the sentence more confusing. In this sentence, where the subject is an undefined person, the pronouns *he, she* or *he or she* would be appropriate.

12. A: In the other version, the subject of the introductory clause is not identified until the end of the sentence. The other version does a better job of presenting the same information.

13. B: In the other version, the word where is used incorrectly. Government oversight is not a place. It would be equally incorrect to begin the sentence with the phrase "Government oversight is when." The correct sentence expresses the same meaning more grammatically.

14. B: The other version of the sentence suggests that magazine journalists are more fair-minded than the newspapers themselves, rather than the people who write for them. In the correct version, the terms of the comparison are clear.

15. B: The other version is unclear as to whether none of the cars were properly registered or not all of the cars were properly registered. In the correct version, the position of *not* makes the meaning plain.

Spelling

16. B: truly

17. A: mischief

18. B: reduction

19. C: candidate

20. C: camouflage

21. A: cartilage

22. B: official

23. A: guarantee

24. C: accumulate

25. D: business

26. A: especially

27. B: excel

28. A: science

29. C: fourth

30. A: labeled

Vocabulary

31. A: *Irritate* most nearly has the same meaning as *aggravate*. Both of these verbs mean to annoy or make uncomfortable.

32. B: *Correct* most nearly has the same meaning as *rectify*. When *correct* is used as a verb, it and *rectify* both mean to set right, to make proper, or to straighten.

33. B: *Embarrass* most nearly has the same meaning as *humiliate*. These verbs refer to making another person feel bad about himself or herself.

34. D: *Con* most nearly has the same meaning as *bilk*. Both of them are verbs meaning to cheat or to take advantage of through trickery or persuasion.

35. A: *Recumbent* most nearly has the same meaning as *supine*. Both of them mean lying down, usually on one's back.

36. D: *Lowering* most nearly has the same meaning as *descent*. Both of these nouns refer to things that are decreasing in elevation or height, or which are getting lower in some other sense. For instance, a person who is beginning to adopt bad habits could be said to be in a descent.

37. B: *Overcome* most nearly has the same meaning as *surmount*. Both of these words mean to triumph over or defeat.

38. A: *Distribute* most nearly has the same meaning as *allocate*. Both of these verbs mean to spread things around or give things out over an area.

39. D: *Recovery* most nearly has the same meaning as *redemption*. Both of these words describe the retaking of a good position after a down period.

40. D: *Reason* most nearly has the same meaning as *rationale*. They both refer to the factors that influence an opinion or decision.

41. B: *Payment* most nearly has the same meaning as *remuneration*. Both of these words refer to the compensation received for work that has been done.

42. A: *Replace* most nearly has the same meaning as *supplant*. *Replace* and *supplant* are both verbs that mean to take the place of or to take over from.

43. C: *Accuser* most nearly has the same meaning as *plaintiff*. Both of these words indicate a person who claims another person has committed a crime.

44. B: *Encourage* most nearly has the same meaning as *incite*. Both of these words mean to spur on, push forward, or motivate.

45. D: *Verdict* most nearly has the same meaning as *decision*. They both refer to choices made after thought or consideration.

Reading Comprehension

46. C: Based on the passage, the most accurate statement is that geographical data can be very useful in law enforcement. The last sentence of the first paragraph states that this data can be combined with police report data "to analyze where, how, and why crime occurs." The passage does not state that criminals are more likely to strike in open areas, but rather that the locations of these areas may affect crime. It seems more likely that criminals would avoid open areas. Finally, the passage does not state that police report data is useless without geographical data, but merely that these data sets can be usefully combined.

47. B: Based on the passage, the most accurate statement is that technological innovation has further increased the utility of geographic data. This is the main idea of the second paragraph. The passage suggests that geographic data has become more influential in recent years, but there is no indication that some geographic data has never been used before. The passage describes how Geographic Information Systems have been used to inform police work, but it does not state that this work has lowered the crime rate. Moreover, there is no suggestion that the causes of crime can all be attributed to geographic factors.

48. A: Based on the passage, the most accurate statement is that public assistance is needed in the fight against terrorism. Indeed, most of the passage is a list of the things one should do to help combat this problem. There is no suggestion in the passage that other countries do not have effective counterterrorism organizations, or that civilians should not be near military facilities under any circumstances. Finally, the passage suggests that terrorists would be more interested in "places where large numbers of people gather," not unpopulated areas.

49. B: Based on the passage, the most accurate statement is that some activities are more suspicious when they occur in particular places. This is clear in the first sentence, which states that some activities indicate possible terrorist plans "especially when they occur" at certain spots. The passage does not state that every FBI Field Office contains a Joint Terrorism Task Force, but rather that every Joint Terrorism Task Force is located within an FBI Field Office. The passage never recommends that citizens try to apprehend suspects themselves. Also, the passage does not state that a large number of people tend to gather at utility stations, though it does include utilities in its list of "high-profile sites or places where large numbers of people gather." It seems more likely that a utility is an example of a high-profile site.

50. C: Based on the passage, the most accurate statement is that crime pattern theory focuses on the relationship between crime and place. The passage describes how certain crimes are more common in those places where they are easier to commit. The passage uses suburban burglaries as an example, but it does not suggest that the theory is only

concerned with this area. Also, the passage does not place responsibility on the neighborhood watch, nor does it state that crime pattern theory only applies to minor offenses.

51. C: Based on the passage, the most accurate statement is that a footprint on a carpet would be an example of impression evidence. Impression evidence, according to the passage, is "created when two objects come in contact with enough force to cause an 'impression.'" The examples of pattern evidence are taken from shoes, but there is no suggestion that shoes are the most common source of this evidence. The passage does not state that either pattern or impression evidence is more valuable. Finally, it appears that these types of evidence must be examined and analyzed, but there is no indication that they need to be sent off to a state laboratory.

52. A: Based on the passage, the most accurate statement is that forensic examiners can match a shoe to a shoe print. This is described in the second paragraph. There is no suggestion that pattern evidence requires less analysis than impression evidence, or that a left shoe cannot be matched to a right shoe print. Finally, the passage does not suggest that a shoe print is not enough evidence to generate a conviction.

53. D: Based on the passage, the most accurate statement is that the broken windows theory draws a link between minor and major crimes. This theory suggests that areas in which there are many minor crimes will see a disintegration of the social order, which will lead to more major crimes. The broken windows theory would not explain crime in wealthy neighborhoods, since these areas are likely to be well-kept and free of "signs of disorder." The broken windows theory does not argue that vandalism is the worst crime, merely that it may contribute to a culture in which more serious crimes are likely to be committed. The passage does not state that the broken windows theory does not apply to rural areas, and in fact there is no reason to suspect that the theory would not apply there just as well.

54. D: Based on the passage, the most accurate statement is that departmental culture has far-reaching effects in law enforcement. This is evident throughout the passage. The second sentence of the passage asserts that departmental culture is closely tied to how officers interact with the public. It seems likely that the author of this passage would be in favor of departments receiving recommendations from the public, but this point is not made in the passage. Finally, the first sentence states that the primary factor influencing police behavior is the "management and culture" of the department, not the crime rate.

55. A: Based on the passage, the most accurate statement is that an organization should have defined values and principles. This is stated directly in the second sentence of the second paragraph. The passage never states that established policies can then be ignored, and in fact it lists "inspections and audits" as one of the priorities of a well-managed organization. The passage states that it is important to detect misconduct, but it never discusses how long this process lasts in general. Finally, the passage does not indicate that managers should receive preferential treatment: on the contrary, "equal treatment for all members of the organization" is listed as a priority.

56. A: Using the above coding system, the call number C-4-A would signify a drug offense in the northern part of the city during the day shift.

57. B: Using the above coding system, the call number B-0-B would signify a traffic violation in the central part of the city during the swing shift.

58. A: Based on the passage, the most accurate statement is that transnational crime often involves smuggling contraband across national borders. This is evident from the list of common transnational crimes given in the final sentence. The passage does not suggest that transnational crime is most common in Eastern Europe, or that it is restricted to the Internet: in fact, many of the crimes listed involve smuggling physical goods into other nations. Finally, transnational crime by definition is a problem for more nations than just the United States.

59. D: Based on the passage, the most accurate statement is that evidence does not have to be physical material. In the first sentence, evidence is defined as "information or objects." Evidence may be something like a bank record, which is more a piece of data than a material object. There is no suggestion that it is difficult to use dental history in a trial, or that only the prosecution may introduce evidence during a trial. Furthermore, the passage suggests that evidence must be introduced in order to be considered by a jury.

60. B: Based on the passage, the most accurate statement is that teenagers and young adults are more likely than other people to be the victims of gun violence. This is stated directly in the third sentence. The passage does not state that young adults are more likely to commit acts of gun violence. Similarly, it makes no assertion about the leading cause of death among middle-aged citizens. In the last sentence, the passage states that most gun violence occurs "in cities and urban communities."

61. A: Based on the passage, the most accurate statement is that stress can be detrimental to an officer's performance. This is indicated in the final sentence, where it states that some officers with stress-induced fatigue "cannot properly protect themselves or citizens." The passage states that PTSD is associated with an inability to sleep, not excessive sleeping. It does not state that most law enforcement officers suffer from fatigue. The first sentence says that stress can lead to depression, but does not state the opposite.

62. D: Based on the passage, the most accurate statement is that stalking must include multiple episodes. According to the definition given in the second sentence, stalking requires "repeated (two or more occasions)" misconduct. Indeed, one of the key features of stalking is that it is a persistent pattern of threatening and/or unwanted behavior. Stalking does not require that the person be intending to stalk: on the contrary, the passage states that the definition of stalking only requires activities that would "cause a reasonable person fear.'" It is conceivable, then, that a person could be convicted of stalking without ever intending to cause fear. Stalking and domestic violence are not the same crime, in part because the latter requires proximity. Stalking, by contrast, may be perpetrated from a great distance, as in cases of cyberstalking.

63. B: Based on the passage, the most accurate statement is that sending a person flowers could be part of a pattern of stalking, if this is part of a pattern of menacing behavior. Specifically, the passage states that sending unwanted gifts can be a form of stalking. The passage does not assert that stalking must include verbal communication; on the contrary, the behavior may be limited to physical proximity or the posting of defamatory information on the Internet. The passage does not state that most stalking goes unreported by the victims. Finally, physical violence against another person goes beyond stalking, and would be classified as assault.

64. C: Based on the passage, the most accurate statement is that burglary always occurs when at a residence, even when that residence is not a home. Indeed, the passage states that burglary may occur at vacation residences and hotels. The passage does not indicate how often burglary occurs at vacation residences. It does state that a vacation residence may be burglarized, and that the occupant at the time is considered to be the resident. Similarly, burglary can occur at a hotel, with the resident defined as the person who has paid for the room at that time. Finally, the passage does not suggest that there are any situations in which burglary is lawful.

65. C: Based on the passage, the most accurate statement is that a burglary may be committed without a theft taking place. The second sentence of the passage states that "this crime usually, but not always, involves theft." Although the term *burglary* commonly is used interchangeably with *theft*, this passage defines burglary as merely the "unlawful or forcible entry or attempted entry of a residence." A burglary may not be committed where the person entering has a legal right to be present. The passage does not indicate whether a burglary without force is better than a burglary with force. One might guess that this is true, but it is not mentioned in the passage. Finally, breaking into a shed may be considered burglary, but only if the shed is located on premises owned by another person.

Cloze

66. when

67. night

68. of

69. alone

70. from

71. with

72. have

73. drunk

74. call

75. asked

76. While

77. heard

78. be

79. like

80. to

81. would

82. soon

83. hung

84. dog

85. door

86. with

87. under

88. that

89. for

90. heard

91. was

92. any

93. car

94. more

95. door

96. to

97. said

98. house

99. later

100. they

101. tree

102. branch

103. house

104. also

105. into

Reasoning

106. D: The next number in the series is 33. This pattern is just three recurring numbers: 11, 22, and 33. After the 22, then, there would be a 33.

107. A: The word *think* is not like the other three. *Ate*, *ran*, and *jumped* are all in the past tense, while *think* is in the present tense.

108. C: The next number in the series is 64. In this pattern, each successive number is twice the previous number.

109. C: A snake is not like the other three. Hamsters, cats, and bears are furry, but snakes are not.

110. D: Victor scored a 95 on the exam. If Sandra scored a 92 and Terry scored seven points lower, then Terry scored an 85. If Victor scored ten points higher than that, he would have scored a 95.

111. B: There is not enough information to solve this problem. Since no specific ages are given for any of the three, there is no way to use the information given to find a correct answer.

112. A: The next number in the series is 23. The pattern here is 23 followed by a number increasing by ten each time. Since the previous term was 64, the next will revert to the 23.

113. D: The word *gnaw* is not like the other three. Sip, gulp, and drink are all actions one would perform with a beverage, while gnawing is something one would do with food.

114. B: Ben won the race. If Andrew finished after Ben but before Carl, then Carl also finished after Ben. If Dan finished in between Carl and Andrew, then there is no chance he could have finished before Ben.

115. C: The next number in the series is 10. This is a pattern of three recurring numbers: 4, 7, and 10. Therefore, a 10 will follow the 7.

116. A: Grace is nineteen years old. If Melanie is seventeen, then Nora is 22. If Grace is three years younger than Nora, then she is nineteen.

117. B: The word *rock* is not like the other three. A tree, person, or flower can grow, but a rock cannot.

118. C: The next number in the series is 673. In this pattern, each of the digits moves back a position each time, with the last digit becoming the first. Therefore, 736 would be followed by 673.

119. C: Paul scored an 88. If Ned scored an 85, and Paul scored three points higher, then he scored an 88. It is not necessary to calculate Oscar's score to solve this problem.

120. C: The next number in the series is 91. In this pattern, the numbers are in a pattern of three, in which the second number is nine less than the first, and the third is twelve less than the second. However, in each successive group of numbers, each term increases by one. So, if 100 begins a new group, the next term will be 91.

121. A: The word *tongue* is not like the other three. Belts, shoes, and hats are all articles of clothing, and a tongue is not.

Secret Key #1 - Time is Your Greatest Enemy

Pace Yourself

Wear a watch. At the beginning of the test, check the time (or start a chronometer on your watch to count the minutes), and check the time after every few questions to make sure you are "on schedule."

If you are forced to speed up, do it efficiently. Usually one or more answer choices can be eliminated without too much difficulty. Above all, don't panic. Don't speed up and just begin guessing at random choices. By pacing yourself, and continually monitoring your progress against your watch, you will always know exactly how far ahead or behind you are with your available time. If you find that you are one minute behind on the test, don't skip one question without spending any time on it, just to catch back up. Take 15 fewer seconds on the next four questions, and after four questions you'll have caught back up. Once you catch back up, you can continue working each problem at your normal pace.

Furthermore, don't dwell on the problems that you were rushed on. If a problem was taking up too much time and you made a hurried guess, it must be difficult. The difficult questions are the ones you are most likely to miss anyway, so it isn't a big loss. It is better to end with more time than you need than to run out of time.

Lastly, sometimes it is beneficial to slow down if you are constantly getting ahead of time. You are always more likely to catch a careless mistake by working more slowly than quickly, and among very high-scoring test takers (those who are likely to have lots of time left over), careless errors affect the score more than mastery of material.

Secret Key #2 - Guessing is not Guesswork

You probably know that guessing is a good idea. Unlike other standardized tests, there is no penalty for getting a wrong answer. Even if you have no idea about a question, you still have a 20-25% chance of getting it right.

Most test takers do not understand the impact that proper guessing can have on their score. Unless you score extremely high, guessing will significantly contribute to your final score.

Monkeys Take the Test

What most test takers don't realize is that to insure that 20-25% chance, you have to guess randomly. If you put 20 monkeys in a room to take this test, assuming they answered once per question and behaved themselves, on average they would get 20-25% of the questions correct. Put 20 test takers in the room, and the average will be much lower among guessed questions. Why?
1. The test writers intentionally write deceptive answer choices that "look" right. A test taker has no idea about a question, so he picks the "best looking" answer, which is often wrong. The monkey has no idea what looks good and what doesn't, so it will consistently be right about 20-25% of the time.
2. Test takers will eliminate answer choices from the guessing pool based on a hunch or intuition. Simple but correct answers often get excluded, leaving a 0% chance of being correct. The monkey has no clue, and often gets lucky with the best choice.

This is why the process of elimination endorsed by most test courses is flawed and detrimental to your performance. Test takers don't guess; they make an ignorant stab in the dark that is usually worse than random.

$5 Challenge

Let me introduce one of the most valuable ideas of this course—the $5 challenge:

You only mark your "best guess" if you are willing to bet $5 on it.
You only eliminate choices from guessing if you are willing to bet $5 on it.

Why $5? Five dollars is an amount of money that is small yet not insignificant, and can really add up fast (20 questions could cost you $100). Likewise, each answer choice on one question of the test will have a small impact on your overall score, but it can really add up to a lot of points in the end.

The process of elimination IS valuable. The following shows your chance of guessing it right:

Eliminate all but this many choices:	Chance of getting it right:
1	100%
2	50%
3	33%

However, if you accidentally eliminate the right answer or go on a hunch for an incorrect answer, your chances drop dramatically—to 0%. By guessing among all the answer choices, you are GUARANTEED to have a shot at the right answer.

That's why the $5 test is so valuable. If you give up the advantage and safety of a pure guess, it had better be worth the risk.

What we still haven't covered is how to be sure that whatever guess you make is truly random. Here's the easiest way:

Always pick the first answer choice among those remaining.

Such a technique means that you have decided, **before you see a single test question**, exactly how you are going to guess, and since the order of choices tells you nothing about which one is correct, this guessing technique is perfectly random.

This section is not meant to scare you away from making educated guesses or eliminating choices; you just need to define when a choice is worth eliminating. The $5 test, along with a pre-defined random guessing strategy, is the best way to make sure you reap all of the benefits of guessing.

Secret Key #3 - Practice Smarter, Not Harder

Many test takers delay the test preparation process because they dread the awful amounts of practice time they think necessary to succeed on the test. We have refined an effective method that will take you only a fraction of the time.

There are a number of "obstacles" in the path to success. Among these are answering questions, finishing in time, and mastering test-taking strategies. All must be executed on the day of the test at peak performance, or your score will suffer. The test is a mental marathon that has a large impact on your future.

Just like a marathon runner, it is important to work your way up to the full challenge. So first you just worry about questions, and then time, and finally strategy:

Success Strategy

1. Find a good source for practice tests.
2. If you are willing to make a larger time investment, consider using more than one study guide. Often the different approaches of multiple authors will help you "get" difficult concepts.
3. Take a practice test with no time constraints, with all study helps, "open book." Take your time with questions and focus on applying strategies.
4. Take a practice test with time constraints, with all guides, "open book."
5. Take a final practice test without open material and with time limits.

If you have time to take more practice tests, just repeat step 5. By gradually exposing yourself to the full rigors of the test environment, you will condition your mind to the stress of test day and maximize your success.

Secret Key #4 - Prepare, Don't Procrastinate

Let me state an obvious fact: if you take the test three times, you will probably get three different scores. This is due to the way you feel on test day, the level of preparedness you have, and the version of the test you see. Despite the test writers' claims to the contrary, some versions of the test WILL be easier for you than others.

Since your future depends so much on your score, you should maximize your chances of success. In order to maximize the likelihood of success, you've got to prepare in advance. This means taking practice tests and spending time learning the information and test taking strategies you will need to succeed.

Never go take the actual test as a "practice" test, expecting that you can just take it again if you need to. Take all the practice tests you can on your own, but when you go to take the official test, be prepared, be focused, and do your best the first time!

Secret Key #5 - Test Yourself

Everyone knows that time is money. There is no need to spend too much of your time or too little of your time preparing for the test. You should only spend as much of your precious time preparing as is necessary for you to get the score you need.

Once you have taken a practice test under real conditions of time constraints, then you will know if you are ready for the test or not.

If you have scored extremely high the first time that you take the practice test, then there is not much point in spending countless hours studying. You are already there.

Benchmark your abilities by retaking practice tests and seeing how much you have improved. Once you consistently score high enough to guarantee success, then you are ready.

If you have scored well below where you need, then knuckle down and begin studying in earnest. Check your improvement regularly through the use of practice tests under real conditions. Above all, don't worry, panic, or give up. The key is perseverance!

Then, when you go to take the test, remain confident and remember how well you did on the practice tests. If you can score high enough on a practice test, then you can do the same on the real thing.

General Strategies

The most important thing you can do is to ignore your fears and jump into the test immediately. Do not be overwhelmed by any strange-sounding terms. You have to jump into the test like jumping into a pool—all at once is the easiest way.

Make Predictions

As you read and understand the question, try to guess what the answer will be. Remember that several of the answer choices are wrong, and once you begin reading them, your mind will immediately become cluttered with answer choices designed to throw you off. Your mind is typically the most focused immediately after you have read the question and digested its contents. If you can, try to predict what the correct answer will be. You may be surprised at what you can predict.

Quickly scan the choices and see if your prediction is in the listed answer choices. If it is, then you can be quite confident that you have the right answer. It still won't hurt to check the other answer choices, but most of the time, you've got it!

Answer the Question

It may seem obvious to only pick answer choices that answer the question, but the test writers can create some excellent answer choices that are wrong. Don't pick an answer just because it sounds right, or you believe it to be true. It MUST answer the question. Once you've made your selection, always go back and check it against the question and make sure that you didn't misread the question and that the answer choice does answer the question posed.

Benchmark

After you read the first answer choice, decide if you think it sounds correct or not. If it doesn't, move on to the next answer choice. If it does, mentally mark that answer choice. This doesn't mean that you've definitely selected it as your answer choice, it just means that it's the best you've seen thus far. Go ahead and read the next choice. If the next choice is worse than the one you've already selected, keep going to the next answer choice. If the next choice is better than the choice you've already selected, mentally mark the new answer choice as your best guess.

The first answer choice that you select becomes your standard. Every other answer choice must be benchmarked against that standard. That choice is correct until proven otherwise by another answer choice beating it out. Once you've decided that no other answer choice seems as good, do one final check to ensure that your answer choice answers the question posed.

Valid Information

Don't discount any of the information provided in the question. Every piece of information may be necessary to determine the correct answer. None of the information in the question is there to throw you off (while the answer choices will certainly have information to throw you off). If two seemingly unrelated topics are discussed, don't ignore either. You can be confident there is a relationship, or it wouldn't be included in the question, and you are probably going to have to determine what is that relationship to find the answer.

Avoid "Fact Traps"
Don't get distracted by a choice that is factually true. Your search is for the answer that answers the question. Stay focused and don't fall for an answer that is true but irrelevant. Always go back to the question and make sure you're choosing an answer that actually answers the question and is not just a true statement. An answer can be factually correct, but it MUST answer the question asked. Additionally, two answers can both be seemingly correct, so be sure to read all of the answer choices, and make sure that you get the one that BEST answers the question.

Milk the Question
Some of the questions may throw you completely off. They might deal with a subject you have not been exposed to, or one that you haven't reviewed in years. While your lack of knowledge about the subject will be a hindrance, the question itself can give you many clues that will help you find the correct answer. Read the question carefully and look for clues. Watch particularly for adjectives and nouns describing difficult terms or words that you don't recognize. Regardless of whether you completely understand a word or not, replacing it with a synonym, either provided or one you more familiar with, may help you to understand what the questions are asking. Rather than wracking your mind about specific detailed information concerning a difficult term or word, try to use mental substitutes that are easier to understand.

The Trap of Familiarity
Don't just choose a word because you recognize it. On difficult questions, you may not recognize a number of words in the answer choices. The test writers don't put "make-believe" words on the test, so don't think that just because you only recognize all the words in one answer choice that that answer choice must be correct. If you only recognize words in one answer choice, then focus on that one. Is it correct? Try your best to determine if it is correct. If it is, that's great. If not, eliminate it. Each word and answer choice you eliminate increases your chances of getting the question correct, even if you then have to guess among the unfamiliar choices.

Eliminate Answers
Eliminate choices as soon as you realize they are wrong. But be careful! Make sure you consider all of the possible answer choices. Just because one appears right, doesn't mean that the next one won't be even better! The test writers will usually put more than one good answer choice for every question, so read all of them. Don't worry if you are stuck between two that seem right. By getting down to just two remaining possible choices, your odds are now 50/50. Rather than wasting too much time, play the odds. You are guessing, but guessing wisely because you've been able to knock out some of the answer choices that you know are wrong. If you are eliminating choices and realize that the last answer choice you are left with is also obviously wrong, don't panic. Start over and consider each choice

again. There may easily be something that you missed the first time and will realize on the second pass.

Tough Questions

If you are stumped on a problem or it appears too hard or too difficult, don't waste time. Move on! Remember though, if you can quickly check for obviously incorrect answer choices, your chances of guessing correctly are greatly improved. Before you completely give up, at least try to knock out a couple of possible answers. Eliminate what you can and then guess at the remaining answer choices before moving on.

Brainstorm

If you get stuck on a difficult question, spend a few seconds quickly brainstorming. Run through the complete list of possible answer choices. Look at each choice and ask yourself, "Could this answer the question satisfactorily?" Go through each answer choice and consider it independently of the others. By systematically going through all possibilities, you may find something that you would otherwise overlook. Remember though that when you get stuck, it's important to try to keep moving.

Read Carefully

Understand the problem. Read the question and answer choices carefully. Don't miss the question because you misread the terms. You have plenty of time to read each question thoroughly and make sure you understand what is being asked. Yet a happy medium must be attained, so don't waste too much time. You must read carefully, but efficiently.

Face Value

When in doubt, use common sense. Always accept the situation in the problem at face value. Don't read too much into it. These problems will not require you to make huge leaps of logic. The test writers aren't trying to throw you off with a cheap trick. If you have to go beyond creativity and make a leap of logic in order to have an answer choice answer the question, then you should look at the other answer choices. Don't overcomplicate the problem by creating theoretical relationships or explanations that will warp time or space. These are normal problems rooted in reality. It's just that the applicable relationship or explanation may not be readily apparent and you have to figure things out. Use your common sense to interpret anything that isn't clear.

Prefixes

If you're having trouble with a word in the question or answer choices, try dissecting it. Take advantage of every clue that the word might include. Prefixes and suffixes can be a huge help. Usually they allow you to determine a basic meaning. Pre- means before, post-means after, pro - is positive, de- is negative. From these prefixes and suffixes, you can get an idea of the general meaning of the word and try to put it into context. Beware though of any traps. Just because con- is the opposite of pro-, doesn't necessarily mean congress is the opposite of progress!

Hedge Phrases

Watch out for critical hedge phrases, led off with words such as "likely," "may," "can," "sometimes," "often," "almost," "mostly," "usually," "generally," "rarely," and "sometimes." Question writers insert these hedge phrases to cover every possibility. Often an answer choice will be wrong simply because it leaves no room for exception. Unless the situation calls for them, avoid answer choices that have definitive words like "exactly," and "always."

Switchback Words

Stay alert for "switchbacks." These are the words and phrases frequently used to alert you to shifts in thought. The most common switchback word is "but." Others include "although," "however," "nevertheless," "on the other hand," "even though," "while," "in spite of," "despite," and "regardless of."

New Information

Correct answer choices will rarely have completely new information included. Answer choices typically are straightforward reflections of the material asked about and will directly relate to the question. If a new piece of information is included in an answer choice that doesn't even seem to relate to the topic being asked about, then that answer choice is likely incorrect. All of the information needed to answer the question is usually provided for you in the question. You should not have to make guesses that are unsupported or choose answer choices that require unknown information that cannot be reasoned from what is given.

Time Management

On technical questions, don't get lost on the technical terms. Don't spend too much time on any one question. If you don't know what a term means, then odds are you aren't going to get much further since you don't have a dictionary. You should be able to immediately recognize whether or not you know a term. If you don't, work with the other clues that you have—the other answer choices and terms provided—but don't waste too much time trying to figure out a difficult term that you don't know.

Contextual Clues

Look for contextual clues. An answer can be right but not the correct answer. The contextual clues will help you find the answer that is most right and is correct. Understand the context in which a phrase or statement is made. This will help you make important distinctions.

Don't Panic

Panicking will not answer any questions for you; therefore, it isn't helpful. When you first see the question, if your mind goes blank, take a deep breath. Force yourself to mechanically go through the steps of solving the problem using the strategies you've learned.

Pace Yourself

Don't get clock fever. It's easy to be overwhelmed when you're looking at a page full of questions, your mind is full of random thoughts and feeling confused, and the clock is ticking down faster than you would like. Calm down and maintain the pace that you have set for yourself. As long as you are on track by monitoring your pace, you are guaranteed to have enough time for yourself. When you get to the last few minutes of the test, it may seem like you won't have enough time left, but if you only have as many questions as you should have left at that point, then you're right on track!

Answer Selection
The best way to pick an answer choice is to eliminate all of those that are wrong, until only one is left and confirm that is the correct answer. Sometimes though, an answer choice may immediately look right. Be careful! Take a second to make sure that the other choices are not equally obvious. Don't make a hasty mistake. There are only two times that you should stop before checking other answers. First is when you are positive that the answer choice you have selected is correct. Second is when time is almost out and you have to make a quick guess!

Check Your Work
Since you will probably not know every term listed and the answer to every question, it is important that you get credit for the ones that you do know. Don't miss any questions through careless mistakes. If at all possible, try to take a second to look back over your answer selection and make sure you've selected the correct answer choice and haven't made a costly careless mistake (such as marking an answer choice that you didn't mean to mark). The time it takes for this quick double check should more than pay for itself in caught mistakes.

Beware of Directly Quoted Answers
Sometimes an answer choice will repeat word for word a portion of the question or reference section. However, beware of such exact duplication. It may be a trap! More than likely, the correct choice will paraphrase or summarize a point, rather than being exactly the same wording.

Slang
Scientific sounding answers are better than slang ones. An answer choice that begins "To compare the outcomes..." is much more likely to be correct than one that begins "Because some people insisted..."

Extreme Statements
Avoid wild answers that throw out highly controversial ideas that are proclaimed as established fact. An answer choice that states the "process should used in certain situations, if..." is much more likely to be correct than one that states the "process should be discontinued completely." The first is a calm rational statement and doesn't even make a definitive, uncompromising stance, using a hedge word "if" to provide wiggle room, whereas the second choice is a radical idea and far more extreme.

Answer Choice Families
When you have two or more answer choices that are direct opposites or parallels, one of them is usually the correct answer. For instance, if one answer choice states "x increases"

and another answer choice states "x decreases" or "y increases," then those two or three answer choices are very similar in construction and fall into the same family of answer choices. A family of answer choices consists of two or three answer choices, very similar in construction, but often with directly opposite meanings. Usually the correct answer choice will be in that family of answer choices. The "odd man out" or answer choice that doesn't seem to fit the parallel construction of the other answer choices is more likely to be incorrect.

Additional Bonus Material

Due to our efforts to try to keep this book to a manageable length, we've created a link that will give you access to all of your additional bonus material.

Please visit http://www.mometrix.com/bonus948/calipost to access the information.

Made in the USA
San Bernardino, CA
28 March 2018